THE SWORD AND A PEN

12 Lessons for Christian Writers

Lisa Bell

Cover design by Radical Women

For discounts on group purchases or to request the author as a speaker, please contact the publisher.

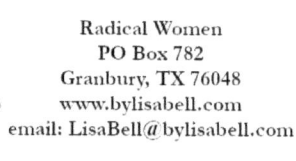

Radical Women
PO Box 782
Granbury, TX 76048
www.bylisabell.com
email: LisaBell@bylisabell.com

ISBN: 9798988648567

For the Heights Church in Granbury.
You allowed me to share my writing gifts and skills,
and this book came from the first small group.

"The biggest mistake you will ever make—is living with the fear of making mistakes."
                    - Dietrich Bonhoeffer

Table of Contents

Acknowledgments

Thank you, Dee Dee Ward, Erica Howard, and Eva Cortes. The three of you met weekly, showing grace as I presented new material, which became part of this book. In many ways, your questions, discussion, and encouragement helped create the content. I look forward to the books and other work coming from our small group of aspiring new writers. Your stories and enthusiasm for writing compelled me to revisit skills and make sure I gave you my best so you can grow into amazing writers, as I know you all will.

Andy Ward, thank you for letting us disturb your Sunday afternoons and at times giving us feedback and your wonderful sense of humor. And of course, we can't forget your ready invitations to go out for lunch and dinner every Sunday.

Pastor Daniel, thank you for encouragement to use our gifts and for your support. All Heights pastors truly encourage us to share our gifts and talents as small-group leaders, but in a world where many churches talk about equipping, you enable serving. For that, I am grateful.

As always, thank you to Heart & Soul Writers and Living Waters Writers for feedback on content as I prepared to lead these new writers and develop a tool for them. You keep me humble and accountable in so many ways. Without you, I wouldn't know half of what I do about writing, and I wouldn't continue improving and remembering the many facets of making our words the best we possibly can.

The Sword and a Pen

12 Lessons for Christian Writers

Introduction

Having written for over a decade, I spent much of that time working as first a freelance writer and then as a local magazine editor. At the same time, I offered freelance editing and publishing assistance for writers. Many times, people told me, "I have written a book." Sometimes, they said, "I feel like God told me to write a book, but I don't know where to start."

As a Christian, I wanted to keep Jesus in my writing without preaching or boring readers. Although a Christian woman owned the magazine I worked for, we often got reminders about it being a secular magazine. Which meant I learned to talk about Jesus without putting Him in the readers' faces. I loved when people quoted the Bible or brought God or Jesus into the interview. When we write as Christians, we may make it all about Jesus, refer to Bible verses, quote scripture — or not. We can choose to share Jesus indirectly. Much depends on our readership. We'll get into that more during these next 12 weeks.

When I first submitted to a call on my life to write and teach, I had no clue what I didn't know about writing. After all, I started writing at 6 years old — didn't we all? All joking aside, people often told me I wrote well. Still, it took years of conferences, workshops, seminars, and critique groups to have half-a-clue about the how-to of book writing. Not all writers want to take that long journey of writing a book. Some want to write other things — articles, devotionals, so much more. While you need to know what you desire to write, the lessons in this workbook apply to most any writing. We'll look at both fiction and non-fiction.

Back to the provocative question. How do I begin?

In 2022-2023, I sensed a need for a class that hit on the high points of writing with the added benefit of biblical inspiration and instruction in the process. Thus, a journey into this course began for me. As a member of The Heights Church in Granbury, Texas, I vetted these 12 lessons, knowing the content might change.

Although created for a church small group, it can benefit an individual who wants to learn. However, writing tends toward solitude, and it can become a lonely road for many writers. By incorporating these lessons into a small-group setting, the writers support, encourage, and challenge one another.

This is not a book for mere reading, but one that challenges the writer to take steps toward completing a project—whatever that looks like to you. From beginner to advanced writer, we need each other. Hence, we write together, yet alone.

Are you ready for a journey to learn, remember, or assist others? Then let's go.

"And let us consider how to stir up one another to love and good works." (Hebrews 10:24 ESV)

The Sword and a Pen

12 Lessons for Christian Writers

"Jesus said to pray for more harvest laborers, which says we need more Christians writing for the general market, where our stories contain biblical truth without mentioning the Bible, God, or Jesus." Frank Ball

"The world does not need more Christian literature. What it needs is more Christians writing good literature." C. S. Lewis

"I am a Christian and of course what I write will be from that essential viewpoint." J.R.R. Tolkien

Lesson 1—The W's of Writing

Focal verse for lesson one: "The one who believes in Me, as the Scripture said, 'From his innermost being will flow rivers of living water.'" John 7:38 (NASB)

Lesson 1 Introduction

Jesus spoke these words, which assures us we will produce rivers of living water from deep within if we believe in Him. What does this verse have to do with writing? Everything.

The word translated from Greek as innermost being (koilia) means belly or womb. I find that fascinating since most authors call books their babies. Having written books, it often feels like months of a child growing inside. And birth only initiates a new phase—marketing that baby. We coddle it and pray everyone loves what God gave us to share.

Whether writing a book, an article, a devotional, blog, or whatever, the desire to write comes from God's prompting to release those rivers of living water. Over the next weeks and months, we'll look at this art of writing, what we can accomplish with it, and how to keep Jesus as our focus.

David Mathis, editor for Desiring God, wrote, "God has spoken, so we speak. God has written, so we write—not to eclipse God's words but to illumine them, explain them, celebrate them, and offer them to others." [1]

Whatever we choose to write as Christians, we do it to glorify God. Does that mean we can only write inspirational or Bible studies? Of course not. While the world may need these types of books, Jesus instructed us to reach others with the Gospel and to make disciples. While biblical books help, they don't necessarily draw unbelievers. But that's where we must understand exactly what God calls us to write and follow Him in obedience.

One last thought, because I am a Christian, everything I write is Christian, even if I never mention Jesus. A non-believer does not write Christian works, no matter how many times he or she invokes the name of Jesus.

Let's start this lesson with Scriptures for writers.

What does the Bible say about writing?

Look up these references and record what Holy Spirit speaks to your heart.

- 2 Timothy 3:16-17
- Exodus 17:14
- Joshua 18:4
- Ecclesiastes 12:10
- Jeremiah 30:2
- Luke 1:3
- Revelation 1:11
- Revelation 21:5

Many times, in the Bible, we see express instructions to write. Imagine if no one ever wrote all the stories, history, and instructions that comprise today's Bible. Not that we should be part of the Bible, but in the same way, we can impact lives by using the gift and talents God gave us for writing.

---

[1] (Mathis 2017)

Prayer: Lord, as we learn more about writing, create a desire within each of us to bring glory to you through the words we pen. Make our paths clear and create in us a desire to give our very best to whatever You desire to flow from our innermost being.

Why write?

The single most important part of writing comes from understanding your why. If you don't know why you write, when times get difficult (and they will get difficult) the temptation to quit can overwhelm you. If you get nothing else from this course, answer this question. Why do you write or want to write?

_____

_____

_____

_____

_____

_____

_____

_____

_____

_____

_____

_____

_____

What will you write?

While we have many choices for writing, we need to consider what to write. Books, articles, letters, blogs. Fiction or non-fiction — the genre within the major category. While this can feel daunting, answering this question helps determine what comes next. Although some say you cannot be successful with both fiction and non-fiction, I disagree. Focus on learning and perfecting the one you most want to write, knowing the Lord may ask you to write something other than what you expect. What you read most generally determines what you may write best, but not always. Be open to

Holy Spirit leading you in various directions. What do you write or want to write?

_____

_____

_____

_____

_____

_____

_____

_____

_____

_____

Who will you write for?

Ultimately, we write for an audience of One. Okay, cliché, but true. We seek not to please men, but to please God (Galatians 1:10). Still, knowing your target reader determines how you write. Children's picture books look and sound far different from an adult literary work. Inspirational works for a 30-year-old man don't work for a 50-year-old woman. Get the point? Avoid saying, "Oh, I write for everyone." We must learn to write in specific ways depending on those we want to read our work. Who do you see as your target audience?

_____

_____

_____

_____

_____

_____

_____

_____

_____

When will you write?

For most writers, time constraints affect our ability to write. We have lives, jobs, family, friends. And when we commit to glorify God with our talent, the enemy will do his best to devour every ounce of time allocated to following that commitment (1Peter 5:8). "Oh, I'll write when the mood strikes." If you have that attitude, you'll write little. Not to say that you shouldn't stop and write if you suddenly have the urge. Do it! Serious writers plan writing times. We don't always keep those plans, but we at least try.

Most write daily—at least for 30 minutes. Some set aside weekly writing sessions to make progress. Consider time away for a weekend of nothing but writing—either individually or corporately. Attributed to Benjamin Franklin, "If you fail to plan, you plan to fail." Because life gets in the way of writing, determine a plan to mitigate this weakness. Answer this question and choose to honor it as a commitment to yourself and God. When do you plan to write?

_____

_____

_____

_____

_____

_____

_____

_____

_____

_____

_____

Where will you write?

Like planning a time, knowing where you can steal away to write can make a massive difference. While we don't require an "office" or "study," it certainly doesn't hurt. Trying to write with a TV in the background may work for you, but it can also become a major distraction.

Consider a semi-permanent place for the bulk of your writing. Retreating to you spot shifts your mind into writing mode. That doesn't mean you always go there. A trip to a coffee shop might shake a block loose. Taking a laptop outside might inspire something new. This writing place has flexibility, as it should. View writing as art, because it is. Serious artists have studios, and as writers, we may need one, too. If all you have is the kitchen table or breakfast bar, go for it. Use whatever works for you, but think this through. Give yourself permission to dream of a writing studio. Maybe not when you begin, but perhaps later.

Where do you plan to write?

_____

_____

_____

_____

_____

_____

_____

_____

_____

_____

_____

What place does Jesus take in your writing?

Much of this depends on your target audience. Christian readers expect to see Jesus and biblical references and words. Non-Christians readers require a subtler approach. Neither group wants you to preach at them, and many Christians do not truly know the Bible, neither do they necessarily hold it as the ultimate truth. Shocking, but sadly true. Keep in mind, even Christian readers may not have grown up in church, so using churchy words may prove confusing for them.

While you understand terms like saved, born again, etc., these words may confuse readers. Those who attend church regularly may not have a personal relationship with Jesus, so avoid making that assumption.

As you consider this question, explore how you want to present Jesus in your writing. A wonderful example, *The Fred Factor* by Mark Sanborn, taught biblical principles. Mark didn't mention Jesus until the end of the book, though. Consequently, people read this book that might never have picked up a "Christian" book.

This question has no right or wrong answer. Novelist Jessica Patch weaves Jesus into her stories in the books *Her Darkest Secret* and *A Cry in the Dark*. But not all her characters are Christians, and those who are admit their weaknesses. She allows characters to admire, although not embrace, the Christians in her stories.

In your writing, determine which approach you plan to take. Record your thoughts and see where you go from there.

_____
_____
_____
_____
_____
_____
_____
_____
_____
_____
_____

Where do I go from here?

Many people want to write their story or feel a tug to write something God gave them. But they do not know how to get from "I want to write…" to the process of writing. In the writing world, you hear two terms — plotters and panzers. Regardless of genre or type of writing, you encounter these two extremes. The word outline drums up memories of English classes and the boring task of creating one. Most students cringe at that thought, although some of us enjoyed the organization of ideas, and we saw the value of putting a plan on paper. Pantzers fly by the seat of their pants with a loose idea of start and finish, but nothing recorded for reference. They declare, "My characters write the story as we go."

Perhaps most writers fall between the two extremes. A plot or outline keeps us on track, but it can never become so stagnant we won't let a manuscript grow or change from that initial step of planning. Do you have to do this step? Not necessarily. However, would you take a trip without a map? Yeah—I'll just employ GPS. What if GPS fails? What if you lose your connection? Then you end up in the middle of nowhere wondering if it is the place of horror movies.

In lesson two, we look at a book concept and the dreaded O and P words (Outline and Plotting). Some place O and P in their list of curse words, never spoken or written. Others consider them a lifeline. You get to determine which fits your style and how deep you want to go with these.

So where do you start when facing the daunting task of writing? Short answer—begin with writing your concept. Not only does this focus your thoughts, but it also provides the basis of your back-cover copy. Next, consider what goes into the book—events, topics, plotline, etc.

For this lesson, write one sentence that describes your book. In the next lesson, we will build on that sentence.

_____

_____

_____

_____

_____

_____

_____

_____

_____

_____

Lesson 1 Homework: If you didn't finish answering all the questions in this lesson, finish them before moving forward with lesson two. Jot down any questions you have from lesson one or that arise during the week.

Suggested Resources: *The First 50 Pages* by Jeff Gerke.

Further reading: www.desiringgod.org/articles/god-made-you-a-writer

The Sword and a Pen

12 Lessons for Christian Writers

"God can carry on his own work, though all such poor tools as I were broken." Karen Swallow Prior

"Don't be afraid to really use your imagination. Let it run wild. It's one of the most powerful tools you've got." Laird Hamilton

"Don't let your tools become your process." Anonymous

Lesson 2—In a Book's Beginning: Writing in Action

Focal verse for lesson 2: "Whatever you are doing, work at it with enthusiasm, as to the Lord and not for people." (Colossians 3:23 NET).

Lesson 2 Introduction

In biblical days, men wrote on stone tablets with—I have no idea. But obviously from verses in the Bible, they wrote on something with something. Imagine having to do that? Later, as humanity progressed, we graduated to pen and paper, which made writing a bit easier. Then, the glory of a typewriter. Most of us type faster than we write, so it became a musical way to write—the tap, tap, tap of keys hitting the paper and the warning ding and zip of the return. Oh, the beauty of White-Out and correction tape. Still, if you made mistakes, correcting them didn't come easy. And Lord help if you had to change a scene or rewrite a paragraph. You might have to retype an entire manuscript. I wonder if that's when authors chose chapter breaks?

In the 1990s, the life of writers changed exponentially with the advent of personal computers. At our fingertips, literally, we had word processing abilities with the glorious invention of inserting new text, deleting entire passages, and simply adding the revised words. And software improved, so the computers learned to catch our grammar and spelling errors. What an amazing thing for those of us who prefer spending our time simply writing and not worrying about all that extra work.

These days, we have many tools at our disposal, and no writing course should ignore them. While we won't go into deep detail, we will take a brief look at some tools which can make your writing life easier.

(Disclaimer: this is not an exhaustive list; other tools exist and new software launches frequently. Be open to reviewing tools when you discover them.)

Every career or hobby offers tools, some critical, some important, and some nice to own. Not every tool fits every writer, so this list comes with another warning — just because one writer likes a specific tool doesn't mean you have to like it, too. And if you prefer simple, familiar tools, go for it. These mentioned below represent tools used by many writers, but rest assured, numerous writers stick with MS Word or something compatible.

Tools for Writing

Some people love curling up on a sofa or overstuffed chair with a spiral notebook, legal pad, or perhaps a composition book. These make fantastic places for recording ideas, brainstorming a story, and a gazillion other things writers do. In truth, you may find writers perusing the aisles of the back-to-school areas in any store, and most of us admittedly love seeing the clearance signs announce a bargain on these items.

While a paper and pencil or pen record words, at some point you must create an electronic file, however. No publisher will accept a handwritten manuscript. Neither will most editors — if they do, they have someone who types it for them and you get to pay the bill. Keep that in mind.

So, what do we use to create this magical file referred to as a manuscript (or MSS)?

- ❖ MS Word — the #1 choice for many writers, editors, and publishers.
- ❖ Scrivener — a writing tool, with more options and possibilities than MS Word.
- ❖ Atticus — not the best for writing, although they keep improving options, it produces beautifully formatted books for those who publish themselves.
- ❖ Any other program that creates a readable file (docx, rtf, txt, etc.).

These are examples of programs you can use to transform your words into a file you can save and submit. Each has pros and cons. We'll briefly discuss these.

Most people have MS Word or something similar on their computers. Because this is the most-used program amongst editors and publishers, it works well. It also has a host of formatting capabilities (like page or section breaks; header styles; built-in table of contents and reference tools; and so much more). If you never have taken a class on using MS Word, consider doing so. (A document is available as a quick reference guide to headers, table of contents, and reference tools at www.texasradicalwriters.com.)

MS Word has limitations, but it works well for those who write start to finish. You can save each chapter as a separate document and combine later. This method works if you aren't sure of the order when you begin, or you write chapters in a random order. If you have Windows 10 or 11, you can also utilize voice to text. (Press and hold the windows key and click h — a mic pops up. When it notifies you "listening," say what you want and watch it appear in your document.)

In addition to word processing capabilities, Scrivener provides a single place to store research, organize, reorganize, write and even format your manuscript. Although you may need to watch tutorials to understand how to use it, once you learn the software, it may become your favorite tool for writing. It works well for both fiction and non-fiction and makes it simple to rearrange scenes or chapters. A powerful tool, many authors prefer Scrivener for writing. Think of it as a super-sized binder where you can keep everything together. You can use it with macOS, Windows, or iOS. Other tools integrate with this software, and you can export files as various document types for sending or sharing with others.

At the end of 2023, a onetime fee of $59.99 [$23.99 for iOS (iPad, etc.)] makes it an affordable option. The fee includes any updates to newer versions.

Available at www.literatureandlatte.com/scrivener/overview.

Fairly new and created by people who work primarily with self-publishers, Atticus allows you to export as a docx file type (but you may lose formatting), a PDF, and ePUB (for digital books — AKA Kindle, Nook, etc.). Atticus offers some amazing formatting options that make books unique. Although you can use it for writing a book, and I'm sure some do, it lacks options you can find in other software. However, they continue making constant updates, listening to their customers. And they offer fantastic tutorials to watch. For prolific writers who plan to publish independently, it can save considerable time in creating uploadable files for books. It also provides beautifully crafted books without paying a graphic artist or publishing assistant to design your book interior.

(Onetime fee of $147, it works with both MAC and Windows. www.atticus.io.)

These are three options, but the sky's the limit. You can use open software to create a document, perhaps Google docs, or something like that. Just be sure you can download to a file compatible with Word docx. Otherwise, you'll have difficulties finding an editor, agent, or publisher who wants to work with you.

Other Tools for Writers

- ❖ Grammarly (tool for checking grammar, spelling, and some style).
- ❖ ProWritingAid (similar to Grammarly but with many more options to help improve your writing).
- ❖ Plottr (visual software that assists with development of your book—Plottr offers a tool for character sketches, plotting, world-building, tracking a series, and tons more. It also integrates with Word and Scrivener. They provide tutorials and often host free webinars related to writing that may or may not include using the tool.)
- ❖ E-Sword (amazing tool for Bible study—free to download and use, it comes with limited versions of the Bible. You can add free reference books or purchase other Bibles and resources at reasonable prices. It also has a scripture memory tool. Highly recommend this as a resource for anyone who writes biblical books, articles, etc. Really, for any Christian who wants to dig deeper into the Bible.)
- ❖ Nitro (PDF reader and creator—free version available or you can upgrade to PRO for less than Adobe.)
- ❖ KDPRocket (Tool to assist with marketing.)

These tools are optional, although they can help in dozens of ways with making writing easier and better. Do NOT feel you have to acquire all of them. You may not want any of these software tools, and that's okay.

Every day, techies create new software, a few directed toward writers. Some cost far too much for many writers, and others do what something else does. So don't get caught up in needing to use every tool available. Find what works best for you and use that one (or five, or six, or ten). You may find others online; these are personal favorites I use consistently in writing and related activities.

Of the tools listed, which sounds like your preferred tool for writing and why? Which might you want to explore more?

_____

_____

_____

_____

_____

_____

_____

_____

_____

_____

With that out of the way, let's move on to creating a book concept.

Book Concepts

At the end of Lesson One, we wrote one sentence to describe our book. (Note: this method comes from Randy Ingermanson and *The Snowflake Method*. It consistently helps me not only with developing books but also in honing the back-cover copy.)

Go back to the one sentence. Expand that sentence into a paragraph about your book.

_____

_____

_____

_____

_____

_____
_____
_____
_____
_____

Third, take each sentence in that paragraph and write a paragraph to develop that thought.

_____
_____
_____
_____
_____
_____
_____
_____
_____
_____
_____
_____
_____
_____
_____
_____
_____
_____
_____
_____
_____
_____
_____
_____
_____

_____

_____

_____

Finally, summarize those sentences into about 50-75 words.

_____

_____

_____

_____

_____

_____

_____

_____

_____

Congratulations! You just developed a book concept.

This method helps focus your attention on a single idea for the book, but it also expands that idea enough to fill the pages of a book. As you write, you can always return to this concept for clarification and to keep yourself on track.

If you do nothing else when preparing to write, take time to do these steps. Even if writing articles, newsletters, series of articles, or blogs, this method gets blood flowing to the brain and thoughts focused. Trust the process.

The O and P Words

Now that you have a concept, or at least the beginnings of one, let's move to the next step in writing.

Outline and Plotting conjure memories of high-school themes, essays and research papers. Maybe that's why so many writers consider them four-letter words. Honestly, creating an outline or working through a plot for a novel feels like so much busy work when I want to write those life-changing words. The content burns within me, not an outline or plot.

However, outlining or plotting can provide the best tools to keep you on track, avoiding the dreaded writers' block. Consider at least a high-level, loose and flexible outline for non-fiction, or for fiction, jot down the structure of your plotline. You have one — even if it exists only in your head. *Homework: Create a high-level outline or plot for your project.*

Genre Specifics

In today's world, multiple genres exist no one heard of even a decade ago. "Though we're only covering 35 of the most popular in this post, there are around 50 genres in total — the exact number depends on who you ask. If you take subgenres into account, over on Reedsy Discovery we have 107 different categories, while Amazon has over 16,000!"[2]

This list doesn't include the ever-growing Romantic Suspense or others. Why does it matter? When pitching to a traditional publisher or agent, they want to know the genre. For one thing, they don't all publish every genre. If you choose to self-publish, you must select the categories for your book.

Even if you write articles, short stories, or something else, you need to have an idea what you write. And yes, you can pursue more than one genre, but you may choose to perfect one before moving to something different.

Using www.blog.reedsy.com/book-genres/ as a guide, determine which genre(s) and sub-genres your project fits. It may fit into more than one.

_____

_____

_____

Research

Research plays such an important role in writing — as true for fiction as non-fiction. Have you ever read a book that disappointed you because of something you knew wasn't true? When writing non-fiction, poor research

---

[2] (Reedsyblog 2020)

calls your credibility into questions. For fiction, it may cause you to lose readers.

Depending on what you write, be sure to conduct research before, during, and after your first draft. The slightest error can cause a reader to lay down your book and never finish it. Learn the proper way to cite resources. Putting a website link in your MSS is not a proper footnote or citation if you quote from that source. *(Note: if using MS Word, the software has built-in reference tools to make this simple and to create a bibliography at the end. If you want to list references for a novel, consider using endnotes instead of footnotes.)*

Refer to the document at www.texasradicalwriters.com/resources for instructions on using footnotes and endnotes.

Be cautious with sources. Wikipedia provides tons of information, but many do not consider it a legitimate source because anyone can change it. Rely on truly expert websites, books, magazines, etc. Conduct interviews with those who know your subject. Write what you know, and even then, back your knowledge up with well-known sources.

When considering the setting for a novel, how well do you know the area you plan to use for setting? If it's been many years since you visited a town or state and you set your story in contemporary times, consider a road trip. Places change, and by putting an old restaurant that closed 20 years ago in your story, you lose realism. It's okay to use imaginary places (towns, businesses, etc.), but in mentioning a town, keep it real.

Finally, a word of caution for quoting scripture. No matter how well you know the verse and its address, double-check yourself — not just once, but several times. An editor will only check your accuracy if you ask, and most likely pay them extra, for verification.

What research do you need for your project? Jot down a list of definite or potential subjects you need to study.

_____

_____

_____

_____

_____

_____

_____

_____

_____

_____

World Building

While we think of world building as mostly for sci-fi, fantasy, or dystopian novels, creating a world can apply to any book. Even non-fiction. For example, a book about angels requires a world where we see angels. Can you create that for your reader? We'll talk about show don't tell in coming weeks, but for now. Image the world in your book.

Any novel takes place in a specific setting. It may be your hometown in the 1970s or a current city today. How do you build that world? Imagine it. Take time to determine how your book world looks, feels, smells, sounds, tastes. Consider where various chapters or scenes occur.

Some writers look online for house plans to create a setting. Others imagine famous people as their characters. Determine what you need to build your world and where you can find what you need. If you take a trip for research or to learn about an area, consider it a writing expense.

Think outside the box and create a world where readers feel they know where your characters live or where your non-fiction chapters occur. (See the resources section for two books you might want in your writers' library.)

What type of world exists in your book?

_____

_____

_____

_____

_____

_____

_____

_____

_____

Example stories and personas (non-fiction) and Character Sketches (fiction).

As one of our last steps of preparation before moving to writing, let's break this section down to non-fiction and fiction. Story captures and keeps the interest of readers. God wired us for story, proven throughout the Bible. Jesus loved telling stories, but the Old Testament records history through stories.

With that in mind, consider what example stories (biblical, personal, or shared) you might include in your book. Next, consider the person who will most likely read your book. Create two or three personas of your readers. What are their ages, gender, lifestyles, jobs, etc? You may not want to get as detailed as a fictional character sketch, but take some time doing this.

For fiction writers, take time to know your character intimately. Please access www.texasradicalwriters.com/resources, and download the character sketch template there. Yes, it contains multiple pages of detail, much of which won't show up directly in your novel. For example, you won't say Joe had a phlegmatic personality type, but knowing that about Joe may help you determine how he reacts to situations.

You don't have to create a character sketch for everyone in your novel, but take time to go through this exercise for the protagonist and antagonist, at least. Add any other major characters. For minor characters, record only critical things—hair and eye color, name, etc. That keeps you on track later so you don't have the same character (a spouse or child) with a different name because you called them something else 10 chapters earlier.

Lesson 2 Homework:

1. Create a high-level outline or at least highlights of a plot. (You may go as deep as you like with this assignment or only hit the high points.) These are flexible documents that will change throughout the process of writing a book. Keep that in mind, but have a good idea where your book is heading.
2. Create two or three personas or complete the character sketches for at least your protagonist and antagonist.

3. Begin any research you need for your book. Be sure to document the source so you can go back to it later if necessary.

4. Come to the small group meeting with a short writing example.

Suggested Resources:

(Reminder: these are not required books, but help better understand the world of writing well. Hint: add them to your Christmas wish list.)

How to Write a Novel Using the Snowflake Method (Advanced Fiction Writing Book 1) by Randy Ingermanson

How to Write a Dynamite Scene Using the Snowflake Method (Advanced Fiction Writing Book 2) by Randy Ingermanson

(Note: you may be able to get the Kindle version of both books on Amazon for $10.98 — look for *Advanced Fiction Writing (2 book series)* Kindle Edition.)

Plot & Structure by James Scott Bell

Websites you may want to visit:

www.thewritersview.groups.io/g/TWV

www.texasradicalwriters.com

The Sword and a Pen

12 Lessons for Christian Writers

"Each week, from a different point of view, you get another look at God, and that's exciting to me." ~Della Reese

"One of the exhilarating parts of falling in love is discovering new things about one another and seeing the world from a different point of view." ~Nicholas Sparks

"One has to take several different shots of a subject, from different points of view and in different situations, as if one examined it in the round rather than looked through the same key-hole again and again." ~ Alexander Rodchenko

"At different times in my life, I met God from a different point of view." ~ T Bone Burnett

Lesson 3—POV (aka Point of View)

Focal verse for lesson 3: "'For My thoughts are not your thoughts, nor are your ways My ways,' declares the LORD. 'For as the heavens are higher than the earth, so are My ways higher than your ways and My thoughts than your thoughts.'" (Isiah 55:8-9 NAS95).

Lesson 3 Introduction

"It's all about perspective." How many times have we heard that statement? I agree with Isaiah—trying to figure out God's perspective takes a lifetime, and then we still don't understand all His ways or thoughts. We can try. Then again, probably why few writers dare write from God's POV.

At one time, authors used a god-like point of view called omniscient. Some still write that way, and we'll discuss that in this lesson along with why not to choose that style.

When you think of POV (or point of view), what comes to mind? Go ahead. Jot down your definition.

_____

_____

_____

Now that we have a good idea of perspective, remember, as Christian writers, regardless of what we write, we strive to capture God's perspective as far as humanly possible.

Jesus said, "But an hour is coming, and now is, when the true worshipers will worship the Father in spirit and truth; for such people, the Father seeks to be His worshipers. God is spirit, and those who worship Him must worship in spirit and truth." (John 4:23-24 NAS95)

When we write, the best way to capture the 'right' words grows from worshiping God before every writing session.

How do you feel about seeking the Lord before writing anything? Do you believe it will help or hinder?

_____

_____

_____

_____

Do you see writing as an act of worship? _____

Consider the scribes from biblical times. Scribes came from the priestly tribe of Levi. Although that doesn't mean all writers are priests, it reminds us to be cautious as writers to present God's truth in accordance with the Bible, whether we evoke the name of Jesus or, like the book of Esther, never mention God, Jesus, or Holy Spirit.

"They were also over the burden bearers, and supervised all the workmen from job to job; and some of the *Levites were scribes* and officials and gatekeepers." (2 Chronicles 34:13 NAS95—*emphasis mine*).

"How can you say, 'We are wise, And the law of the LORD is with us'? But behold, the lying pen of the scribes has made it into a lie." (Jeremiah 8:8 NAS95).

Don't let any of this scare you away from what you believe God called you to do—write. Trust that as you listen to Holy Spirit, He will guide your writing, and He will tell you if you veer from His desires.

That said, let's put on our writer hats and look at POV in the world of writing.

Components of POV

Point of view is really two things:
1. Personage
2. Perspective

The voice with which you tell your story refers to personage (first, second and third). Your perspective character answers, "Whose story is this?" [3]

From school, you probably remember first person, second person, and third person. In 2023, according to Dave Chesson, we have a fourth person view, but it stems from modern society and most likely will be one you never use. I'll include it here as a point of discussion though.

- 1st person POV uses the pronouns "I" and "we."
- 2nd person POV uses the pronoun "you."
- 3rd person POV uses the pronouns "she," "he," "they," and "it."
  - 3rd person limited is when the narrator only knows the thoughts of one person.
  - 3rd person omniscient is when the narrator knows more than the thoughts of just one person.
  - We'll look more closely at these.
- 4th person POV uses indefinite pronouns like "one," "oneself," "someone," "anyone." [4]

First Person POV

Typically used in YA (young adult), SciFi, and Memoir, some authors in other genres may use first person for the protagonist and third person when writing from any other character's perspective. (We'll look at changing POVs later.)

As mentioned above, using "I" or "we" denotes first person. Taking the first-person approach may help write in a deeper POV. If you write from only one character's POV, this can work well, but you must be cautious

---

[3] (Jenkins, 2017)
[4] (Chesson, 2023)

about not popping into another character's head.

Second Person POV

When writing in second person (or fourth), the narrator makes the reader the protagonist. While this POV works well in shorter pieces, like lyrics, poetry, etc., you don't see you, your, or yours much in fiction beyond dialogue. In non-fiction, you often see sentences that leave the word understood but not written.

Examples: Call the police. Read the Bible. Pray for direction.

In these examples, the readers understand it means *you* call the police, *you* read the Bible, *you* pray for directions. But we don't need to write the word for our readers to understand we mean to direct the admonition to them.

A word of caution. Overuse of "you," "your," and "yours" in faith-based books or any non-fiction can feel preachy or accusatory. In these genres, consider switching to first person and relate to your reader by sharing stories using fiction techniques. While you write in first person for a non-fiction book, the reader identifies with you instead of feeling inferior to you. Of course, this also means sharing honestly when writing.

Although some say fourth person comes from the modern world, and that may be true, it always existed in more formal writing. The least used, fourth person feels somewhat stilted and formal. Fine for technical or academic writing, most readers don't identify well with a book written in fourth person.

Example: One may choose to read Scripture daily.

Third Person POV

He, she, it, they appear in most every other genre. The most common way to write, third person determines the voice telling the story. While first person lends itself to an intimate connection between the protagonist and author, with practice any author can learn deep point of view, pulling a reader into the story with him or her.

Within third-person POV, a writer may also choose one of three ways to express that POV.

1. Third person omniscient.

2. Third-person limited.
3. Third person deep.

Although third person omniscient POV can appear in both fiction and non-fiction, it presents several issues. First, we (and our characters) aren't God. We cannot read minds. But the omniscient POV does exactly that. In this way of writing, the narrator tells the story, knowing most everyone's thoughts.

While this used to be the primary way of writing many books, it can get confusing because you change character POV frequently. We'll get to that in a minute. The lack of emotional depth can prevent deep emotional ties, and although easier to write, probably not the best.

Third-person limited POV puts the reader in the character's head. The author must practice becoming the character—writing so the reader feels like part of each scene. When done well, readers become entrenched in the story, and sometimes, the book's world captivates the author, too.

Imagine becoming so much a part of your story you look up and wonder for a moment where you are. It can happen. Usually, that means you left the limited POV and traipsed into a deep POV.

Third-person deep POV provides the most powerful writing and reading experiences.

Have you ever read a book and became so deep into it you felt as if you walked alongside the character? That's writing in a deep POV, and we could spend an entire lesson discuss this one aspect of writing. The coming weeks will provide more instruction on how to achieve this skill. Not easy, this type of book (fiction or non-fiction) draws the reader in and helps keep him or her turning pages to find out what happens next.

Imagine arriving at home to hear about your neighbor having a horrendous wreck. How do you feel?

_____
_____
_____
_____
_____
_____
_____

Now imagine, on your way home you see that wreck, then learn it involved your neighbor. Different feelings?

_____

_____

_____

_____

_____

_____

What if you pass that accident and realize it's not your neighbor, but one of your family members? What feelings might that evoke?

_____

_____

_____

_____

_____

_____

_____

_____

Now imagine yourself being in the car, spinning around, and landing upside down. Would that story (in your deep POV) sound different from hearing about your neighbor having an accident? How so?

_____

_____

_____

_____

_____

_____

_____

_____

The deeper in a POV you write, the more vivid the story becomes to the reader.

Choosing the best POV for your work

To better understand POV, consider seeing through a camera lens. When behind a camera, you only see what's in front of you or in your peripheral vision. You can hear what lies behind you, smell all around — sometimes for a great distance, touch or feel things surrounding you (this includes sensing things unseen), and you can taste sometimes what's in the air. When choosing and writing from a character's POV, write as if that character stands behind a camera. You'll stay in the proper POV much better. We'll talk more in coming weeks about using your five senses and emotions for stronger writing.

In POV, a character can't say or think, "I heard Joe sneaking up behind me," or "Joe sneaked up behind me." The character can hear footsteps. She might smell Joe's cologne and assume it's him. But until she turns and looks, she can't know it's Joe.

Ultimately, as the author, you determine which of these works best. When you read, pay attention to which draws you into a book the most. For me, it is always the deep POV, whether first or third person.

Although not POV, you also need to determine from the beginning whether to use past or present tense. The trend, especially for YA books, uses first person present tense. The biggest issue with that? Trying to stay in present tense doesn't work well for most writers. Few maintain present tense well, because backstory always creeps in, and suddenly you're in past tense without realizing it.

Choose one or the other, but remain consistent. In non-fiction, you might get away with switching tenses. If you find staying in present tense difficult, stick with past tense.

When unsure, consider trying a scene in different POVs and see which feels best. In third person, switching to first person may help to deepen a scene and can work as an excellent exercise.

Multiple POVs

Can I write in more than one POV, or do I have to remain in one character's head for the entire book?

Fantastic question. Short answer — yes. New writers may find sticking with one character's POV easier — two at most. After practicing, you can successfully drift into other POVs, but never do it in the same chapter unless you have a scene break.

Things to remember about POV. When you write from a character's POV (usually the protagonist), the character must be in every scene. How can I know what happened if I wasn't there? A writer switches POV because the main character may not appear in every scene, so I can't write from his or her POV. In that case, I must jump into a different character's POV. To do this, either show a scene break *** or simply start a new chapter.

Where novels used to be 20-25 chapters, we commonly see 50-100 chapters in novels now. Non-fiction—still 10-20 at the most. But we can have a one-page chapter.

Quit hopping around between heads

Commonly called head hopping, changing POV midstream can frustrate and confuse readers. Often when a writer does this, a reader stops reading, thinking, "Wait. Who's the character with these thoughts?" Too much of this, and the book ends up on the shelf or donated to a local thrift shop. Perish the thought!

While we sometimes slip into a different POV accidentally, we strive to avoid this practice of head hopping—also where a critique group and editor help. Someone else may catch our POV issue when we miss it.

Remember to change POV either use a scene break or begin a new chapter. Many writers use chapter breaks, even when it means producing short chapters. Some books have chapters that cover only one or two pages.

The movie *Wonder* does a beautiful job of showing various POVs. Consider watching (or rewatching it) to get an idea of telling a story from different POVs. In a book, we can tell a single scene from multiple POVs. Once an exercise for writers, this practice appears in more novels these days, and if not overused, it can be a wonderful tool for capturing the depth of multiple characters in the book and helping the reader understand more than one of them.

Not just POV, but what's the point?

Writers use POV to convey a story in the best possible way. Why? What is the purpose behind writing? Ted Dekker said, "Without change, you have no story. You only have a series of events."

Story requires change — typically of your protagonist — in non-fiction, the book should invite change in the reader (which in a way represents your protagonist).

One of the best ways I ever heard to capture the essence of story comes from Frank Ball, called SCOOP IT UP. When you figure this out for your main character, you come away with good stories.

Situation:

Character:

Objective:

Obstacle:

Plight:

Insight:

Transformation:

Unresolved Problem:

Consider the story of Jesus' birth. Name various POVs for the nativity story.

_____

_____

_____

_____

_____

_____

As a bonus, choose one or two characters from your list and complete the template for SCOOP IT UP.

Lesson 3 Homework:

1. Select the POV for your project.
2. Complete a SCOOP IT UP template for your main character. For non-fiction, make the reader your main character.
3. Write part of a chapter for your non-fiction book, keeping #2 in mind. For fiction, write a scene with #2 in mind.
   a. Bonus: consider a second type of reader for a non-fiction book, or write the scene from a second POV.

4. Jot down any question that arise about POV.

Suggested reading

Storytelling at its Best by Frank Ball (www.roaringwriters.org/author-frank-ball/)

The Sword and a Pen

12 Lessons for Christian Writers

"Don't tell me the moon is shining, show me the glint of light on broken glass." ~Anton Chekhov

"Show the readers everything, tell them nothing." ~Ernest Hemingway

Lesson 4—Show Don't Tell

Focal verse for lesson 4: "Make your tent larger, stretch your tent curtains farther out! Spare no effort, lengthen your ropes, and pound your stakes deep." (Isaiah 54:2 NET).

Lesson 4 Introduction

As writers, we enlarge our tents with written words. While I may only talk to a handful of people, a book, article, blog, etc., knows no physical limits. When we publish the thoughts and insights God gives us, we can potentially reach far more people than we ever will in person. While I enlarge my tents by teaching others to write and write well, I suspect God may call some of my students to teach or guide others, again stretching the walls. Isaiah 54:2 may not speak specifically to writing, but isn't it a beautiful example of enlarging our tents?

A masterful storyteller, Jesus loved teaching with parables. He used stories the people related to alongside a bit of humor. We don't always see that because we don't understand the culture of biblical times, and let's face it. We lose much in translation from the original languages into English.

Nevertheless, Jesus knew how to captivate his listeners. If we are to share the messages He gives us, we must learn to write stories the best we possibly can.

In the writing world, you don't have to spend much time before you'll hear the words, "Show, don't tell." Great admonishment. Except. What does that mean exactly?

The greatest storytellers bring a tale to life. As you listen, the narrator weaves words into sentences that draw you in, hold your interest, and leave you wanting more when he or she finishes. For the duration, you sit in awe, visualize every word, picturing in your mind the scene the storyteller describes. You're there with the character. You laugh, cry, dodge the flaming arrows. These are elements of a story capable of staying with you long after it ends.

Oh, to write this way.

While telling some scenes of a story works, too much of this makes for a boring book a reader puts down and doesn't finish. Too much telling doesn't pull the reader into the story. Memorable writing begins with the idea of show, don't tell. We'll hit the high points in this lesson, but in coming weeks, we'll discuss how to improve this skill. Interestingly, the better you achieve show, don't tell, the deeper you move into a character's POV.

Here's a simple example that can help you see the progression.

She was angry. (Problem—passive telling.)

Lisa fumed. (Better. No passivity, and it kinda shows instead of telling.) But can we make it stronger?

Lisa slammed the cabinet door, whirling to face Mick. "You'll pay for this."

Which of these three sentences best shows you a scene in the story? Why?

_____

_____

_____

_____

_____

Now, let's look at what this phrase (show don't tell) means and how we can do implement it. In a few sentences, we use strong nouns and power verbs, avoid filters, pull in all five senses plus emotions, and dramatize scenes. I strongly recommend reading *Understanding Show, Don't Tell* by Janice Hardy. In this short book, she does a fantastic job of not only explaining the problem areas, but how to correct them. And she also suggests when telling works better than showing.

Let's look at highlights.

Replace Passive Verbs

Passive verbs indicate telling. Any form of to-be verbs (is, was, were, etc.) give us a giant red flag when we look for ways to improve our manuscripts—true regardless of what we write.

A corporate manager once told me, "Just because it's technical writing doesn't mean it has to be boring. Lose the passives." That admonition stuck with me for more than two decades. I suspect I'll never forget her words. When I went back to my desk that day and read my document again, the number of passive verbs shocked me.

Does that mean I can never use one? No. Sometimes we have no alternative. But most of the time we do. When we take this one piece of advice, replacing passive verbs with active ones, our writing improves 100%. Imagine that. Just one thing, and we improve.

As a sidenote, when you write with passive verbs, the brain works twice as hard to read it. With the subject at the end of the sentence— maybe—the brain literally retraces steps to catch the full meaning. A book filled with passive verbs tires the mental capacity much sooner than one filled with active verbs.

If you want to add more umptf to a sentence, try a power verb—one that evokes a sense of power.

Write a passive statement below. Then change it to an active one. Which sounds better?

_____

_____

_____

_____

Strong Nouns and Adjectives

Instead of weak nouns with an adjective, try a stronger noun. Many say cut adjectives, and sometimes we can. Instead of many people use a crowd. When you need an adjective, use one, not two. Very cold—freezing. If you see old, what picture comes into your head? What if I use antique? Still old, but maybe more valuable? When I write ancient, does that change the picture from simply old?

To apply this with the show, don't tell concept, instead of writing the old woman, what if I use something like, wrinkles permeated her face. Either she's old, or appears so, I notice it as the POV character, and I showed something about not only the old woman, but also the character's mindset, perhaps.

Consider your writing project. How can you make changes to nouns and adjectives to improve your writing?

_____

_____

_____

_____

_____

_____

Filters

Another red flag for telling, remove filters. What's a filter? She remembered... Don't tell me she remembered. Go straight to the memory. A word of caution for memories to avoid an info dump, ease into that memory. Something needs to trigger it. In life, we do this, so why not when writing?

If I walk into a kitchen and smell pumpkin and cinnamon baking, my mind goes back to preteen years when I learned to make pumpkin bread, a family favorite during the holidays. Mom called home and asked me to make a batch many times, and when she came home, and slathered butter on it, delight traveled from her mouth to her eyes.

To move back into the current scene, something needs to snap me out of that memory. Perhaps my memory includes the pumpkin bread not sitting well on her stomach right before she ended up in the hospital for gallbladder surgery. Years later, in my scene, Mom's in the hospital and the beep of the heart monitor pulls me back to the present and angst I have for an ailing mother.

Filters pull the reader out of the story. Most of the time, you need only remove the filter to fix the issue, but it may be an indicator that you should show that scene.

Don't tell me she saw, he watched, they remembered. Simply take me to what she saw, what he watched, what they remembered.

Write with Senses

In the space below, write the five senses.

_____

_____

_____

_____

When writing, consider these five senses. Let your character (fiction) experience these senses during a scene. Not every scene includes all five senses, but write what he or she experiences. Don't tell me. Show me that experience. This takes creativity because you must travel to that scene. Close your eyes and experience the smell of something baking. Let me smell and feel what you smell and feel. That captures showing. And what happens? As your reader, I suddenly smell something from personal experience, and it evokes memories in me. Not only am I with your character, but I'm a child walking into Granny's kitchen. Or I'm that preteen who loved baking for my family, who treasured my mom's moment of pleasure after a hard day at work.

I'm captivated by your writing when it touches my heart in some small way.

(Look for homework from this section.)

Show Emotion

Too often in books, articles, whatever, writers tell emotion. Go back to the example in the introduction of this lesson. To avoid passives, many writers go to the second option. Noun-active verb. Better. Concise. Not very moving, and still tells rather than shows. To show emotion, look at visceral reactions (what happens in the body you can't control), outward actions, facial expressions (to show what a non-POV character feels), body language, etc. The best resource I own for this — _The Emotion Thesaurus_ by Angela Ackerman & Becca Puglisi. These ladies have a series of this type of book, well worth the investment to aid with show, don't tell.

In almost two decades of working with writers, critique groups, and editing, I never see too much emotion in books. Don't fear showing emotion. And yes, you may have tears dripping off your chin while writing a scene, but so will your reader while they read the raw words you dared write.

(Watch for homework for this one too.)

Dramatizing Scenes

Final highlight for show, don't tell. Imagine standing behind a camera as you write a scene. Add in the emotions and internal stuff, then capture what you see through that lens. We'll get more into descriptions and dialogue soon, but know these play a critical role in your writing.

While we no longer have the honor of writing long descriptive passages—today's reader sadly doesn't want that—we can write tight scenes that come alive by making the surrounding scenery come alive. When descriptions become characters (albeit brief, minor characters), we move into a world of showing more than telling. We see this in the first quote for this lesson. The moon glints off broken glass. A dog growling or a wolf howling adds suspense to the moon's action. A baby crying in the distance or a siren tells a different story. What if that moon glints off the diamond on your character's left ring finger? Hmmm. What does that evoke in you?

Wrapping up: What we discussed in this lesson scratches the surface of show, don't tell, but it gives you a beginning. Things to consider and much more to learn. This concept, however, provides the foundation for coming weeks in this course.

What questions do you have about this ominous idea of show, don't tell?

_____
_____
_____
_____
_____
_____
_____

Lesson 4 Homework:

1. Find passive sentences in your writing project. Change them into active ones.
2. Look for adjectives and adverbs in your writing. Can you use stronger nouns and verbs?
3. Find any filtering in your writing and remove it, strengthening the scene as needed.
4. Look for one scene in your writing that feels flat when you read it. Try adding at least one or two senses to strengthen it.
5. Find one place in your project that lacks emotion. Add some. Be prepared to share from #4 and #5.

Suggested Resources and Reading:

Understanding Show, Don't Tell: (And Really Getting It) by Janice Hardy

The Emotion Thesaurus: A Writer's Guide to Character Expression by Angela Ackerman & Becca Puglisi

(Any book in the Ackerman & Puglisi Thesaurus series. Warning: you may want all or most of them. ☺ Put them on your Christmas or birthday wish list.)

"249 Strong Verbs That'll Spice Up Your Writing" by Jerry Jenkins *www.jerryjenkins.com/powerful-verbs/*

Lisa Bell

The Sword and a Pen
12 Lessons for Christian Writers

"Dialogue is like jazz. Dialogue is creative." ~Sam Shepard

"The most real dialogue for me is when I am alone, writing." ~ Peter Handke

"The most important thing in communication is to hear what isn't being said." ~Unknown

Lesson 5—Dialogue, Tags, and Talking Heads

Focal verse for lesson 5: "The words of a whisperer are like dainty morsels, and they go down into the innermost parts of the body… Death and life are in the power of the tongue, and those who love it will eat its fruit" (Proverbs 18:8, 21 NAS95).

Lesson 5 Introduction

Words have power—whether we speak them, write them to someone, or include them in a book. With four young daughters, you can imagine the number of hurtful words that flew between them. Not to put myself on a pedestal, I'm sure I spit a few at them from time-to-time, too. Never intentionally of course, but it happens. We open mouths and out spews whatever we think. We can all work to improve in this area.

Decades ago, I read the book *Silver Boxes* by Florence Littauer. Two things stuck with me from her words. (I paraphrase) "Our words should be like tiny silver boxes wrapped up with a bow." Powerful statement, yes? In this book, she also stated that we need 10 positive words for every negative word spoken to us. [5] How could I keep up with four girls? I couldn't. Instead, I put the onus on them. When they said something hurtful, they had to come up with 10 positives, and it couldn't be, "I like your hair and dress." It had to build back up the character they just shot down. Did it work? Maybe. At least they made sure I didn't hear their negative talk to

---

[5] (Littauer F. , 1989)

41

each other, but our home seemed more at peace.

As writers, we have so much power to share Jesus, and we must never take that lightly. Our characters can use this power for good or evil, too, much as we do in real life. Consider these things as we dive into dialogue.

Hopefully, at this point in our course, you have a concept and basic plot or outline ready and maybe started putting words on paper. If not, consider scheduling 30 minutes and give it your best shot. First drafts always need revision, which means don't worry about perfection. Put some thoughts in black-and-white, knowing you will go back and make them better.

In the past four lessons, we looked at basic preparation for writing and dived in to the show, don't tell mindset. We could spend 12 weeks on that lesson alone, but you should understand the basic concept.

In a brief paragraph, record your understanding of show, don't tell and the benefit of writing this way.

_____

_____

_____

_____

_____

_____

_____

_____

Often writers unintentionally tell with dialogue tags, so we'll address that in this lesson. We'll also look at the grammatically correct format for writing dialogue, how to sound natural with it, and the most effective tags. We'll also look at talking heads. What are they, and how do we avoid them?

Even non-fiction books may include dialogue, and most books need it. Through dialogue, we capture backstory, emotions, and action without scores of telling. Even silent movies included dialogue.

Writers often ask me about foul language in Christian books. Do we use foul language in speaking? What line do we refuse to cross in our lives? Many people who proclaim their Christianity have no issue with watching movies or reading books inundated with the foulest of language, and graphic sex doesn't bother them much. The closer I draw to Jesus, the more these things offend me.

Ultimately, you must determine with Holy Spirit guidance where you stand on these issues in writing. In my opinion, reverting to the same tried-and-true foul language cliches requires less creativity than coming up with something original.

We can do better, and as Christians, we should. Maybe a character talks that way, but another character calls the first one out until he or she changes. Or maybe you simply keep out the potty words altogether.

Proper Formatting of Dialogue

Improper formatting of dialogue can produce some of the worst headaches for editors. Did they quit teaching this in school? Did some teachers do a better job than others? Maybe we took a nap during this lesson. I don't know the answer, and it's more of a rhetorical question, anyway. Most authors get this right, but if you want to appear as an amateur writer instead of a professional, mess this one up.

While I hope none of you have an issue with the how to, I can't ignore the possibility you never learned, forgot, or simply took a shortcut. You'd never do that, though, so if you do it incorrectly, I take it no one told you the proper way to write dialogue.

While this doesn't encompass all we need to learn about dialogue, it is an important piece. For the purposes of making sure we don't include common mistakes, here are six rules of dialogue.

1. Each speaker gets a new paragraph. When speakers change, go to a new paragraph even if you have multiple one-line paragraphs.
2. Indent each paragraph. Use first-line indent in your paragraph setup, and this happens automatically. (If you use spaces between paragraphs, which I don't recommend, that should happen automatically too.) This makes the change in speaker clear.
3. Punctuation for what's said always goes inside the quotation marks. No exceptions to this rule!
4. When dialogue includes multiple paragraphs, leave off the ending quotation mark for each paragraph, but be sure to include it at the beginning of the next paragraph. Add ending quotation marks when the speaking character finishes. (Word of caution: this should

be rare. A character who speaks on and on loses a reader's interest. When communicating in person, how quickly do you lose interest if the other person drones on and on and on and…)

5. When a character quotes someone else, use single quotation marks inside of the double quotation marks.
6. Written well, you can avoid he said, she said tags. More on this in the Tags section.

If you are unsure about your punctuation in dialogue, generally any decent grammar software will pick up errors. Be sure to check for these and correct if present.

Any questions?

Natural Dialogue

Most important avoidance in natural dialogue. Avoid using a conversation to info dump backstory. In real life, would you get with a friend and say, "Remember when…" Well, we might, but we wouldn't go into intense detail at that point. You can say, "This reminds me of…" and briefly mention an incident. Janice Hardy shows good examples of this in *Understanding Show Don't Tell*. Dialogue simply cannot become a dumping ground to tell the reader what happened before. It's not natural, so be cautious with this one.

Keep the back-and-forth conversation between characters as natural as possible. Many times, authors make the mistake of using proper words between the characters. Don't. Unless your character is a prim and proper person. Realistically, college professors only teach with big words or if they want to impress someone. Do those words impress you? Neither will they impress readers.

Use contractions — most of us do when talking. Exception: if you have a character who never speaks with contractions, make sure you do that throughout the book. This can be a wonderful way to capture the essence of a character so the readers know who's speaking by the way he or she talks.

MS Word and other grammar software don't like colloquialisms, but if it rings true for your character, let yourself be okay with it. For example: a cowboy in the south tends to use the word "ma'am," and including it in dialogue makes sense if it fits your character's personality.

Try using voice to text and have a conversation with yourself. (Hold down the windows key ⊞ and press h.) Put yourself in the scene and record a back-and-forth conversation, which may create dialogue that sounds more natural than typing out the words. If you continue having trouble, ask another writer to read your scene and make suggestions.

Using too many dialogue tags makes your dialogue drag. If every sentence needs an attribution, consider using nuances to make your character recognizable. What word does a character repeat? Does he use slang? Does she sound like a Georgia peach? If needed, listen to videos of other regions, or better yet, take a trip to a local coffee shop and simply listen to those around you. Take notes.

Sometimes, the most natural response requires no words. Facial expressions, body language, a raspberry coming from one's lips, the eyes speak a thousand words, etc. You get the picture. The most powerful dialogue may have no words or few. Which leads to my next point.

Keep dialogue at the appropriate length. As mentioned earlier, no one wants to read a two-page monologue. If a character needs to give a speech, okay. Put them on a platform, behind a pulpit, or at the front of a class room. But don't fill the page with nothing but that speech.

Think about it. When someone speaks, do they stand in one place, talking, never moving? No pauses? The best speaker looks at someone in the audience, expecting a nodding head. Yes? Break up even the slightest monologue with actions. (More in the tags section. You can't wait to get there can you?) Best case, try to avoid long monologues. Even in non-fiction, droning on puts your reader to sleep, and unless you're going for that effect, work on interactive dialogue.

One last point on natural speaking. Understand the way people communicate. Men generally use fewer words than women do. Keep that in mind. If your male character trusts someone, though, he may engage deeper. Use that knowledge to show trust. Understand personality types and how they affect communication.

- Powerful Choleric personalities=crisp, quick words in most cases. They won't beat around the bush, but go straight to the point.

- Popular Sanguine personalities=talk to anyone, anywhere. The life of the party, they come across as bubbly, full of life and want to bring everyone surrounding them along to a happy place.
- Perfect Melancholy=matter-of-fact; logical, mostly unemotional.
- Peaceful Phlegmatic=don't rock the boat; peaceful and peacekeepers. Have fun with this one though, because a phlegmatic morphs into the other personality types depending on the situation. Least likely to take on the choleric personality, in a pinch with no one else to lead, they can. [6]

The study of personality types can bring a great deal of fun to your writing and help develop characters to a higher level. You can mess with readers by having a character step out of their normal personality. You can also use it to convey something going on with a character. Imagine the popular sanguine entering a room, sneaking into a corner and not saying a word. Yeah. That doesn't happen. Unless said character received horrible, life-changing news minutes before arriving at the party.

Need a quick review? Visit www.thepersonalities.com/category/the-personalities. Some websites suggest 16 personality types. Yikes! Yes, we all have various things that play into our personalities, but we can stick with the four basics and bring every character to life as memorable beings.

Having taken numerous tests to determine my personality type, Florence Littauer makes it simple to understand and has a series of books if you want to dive deeper. I'll add links at the end of the lesson. For a quick review, visit the link above.

Do you know your personality type? If not, consider investing $4 in Florence's online profile.

What do you think is your personality type? Why?

_____

_____

_____

_____

_____

---

[6] (Littauer, 2023)

Use Effective Dialogue Tags

In many books, authors want to avoid repeating said all the time. So, they use she whispered or he interrupted. Not wrong by any means, but most writing experts say stick with said or asked (when it's a question). And never use an action word in place of said.

Example: She laughed, "You're crazy." Try laughing those two words. Not so easy. Another? He nodded, "I'll be there soon." Can you nod those words?

Now, she might laugh and then say, "You're crazy." She laughed. "You're crazy." The action identifies the speaker, but separate it with a period instead of a comma. Such a common mistake that identifies an amateur writer (and some of these are "bestsellers").

You can use actions to identify a speaker instead of the normal tags. Be cautious with this though, because it can be a tell instead of a show.

All that said, remember, you do not need to include who said the statement on every line. In a natural dialogue flow between two people, a reader should know who said what. Hence the beauty of paragraph breaks, too. It helps the reader know the speaker changed. The back-and-forth, if done well, doesn't leave the reader wondering who said that? If it does, rework your dialogue.

Include several lines of dialogue, then throw in action. Think about your conversations. Do you sit and do nothing while talking? Not likely. We get up, move around, sip coffee, lean forward, lean back... These movements include body language that offers a hint for the reader to understand the character's emotions, too. Leaning back shows relaxed or less engaged. When a character leans forward, you sense he or she just engaged or reengaged, or the other character said something that caught his or her attention.

When interrupting, use the ellipsis. In MS Word, when you enter three periods followed by a space, the software automatically adds the bit of separation. You don't need to say he interrupted. The... tells me he did.

Watch out for Talking Heads

A personal weakness for me, I have to watch this one. I get so caught up in the dialogue I forget to add actions and show the surroundings. The action tags help with this, but we can get lost in the dialogue and forget our reader needs a sense of location. A waitress drops a plate, and the crash gives us a break in the intense dialogue. Our reader catches a breath and comes right back to see what else the characters will say. In an airport, the now boarding announcement can ease our hero out of an awkward situation. The people bumping into you might remind the characters to step closer to the wall and continue talking. Use this one or two sentence breaks to remind the reader of location, situations, etc.

This can also help build tension. An unexpected crash on the patio during a serious conversation temporarily breaks the dialogue. You could go either way at that point. The crash is the cat bumping into a plant, the characters laugh, and the seriousness breaks. Or when they look up, a masked gunman stares back at them, the seriousness of the moment intensifies, and our hero and protagonist hit the floor.

These not only break up the dialogue so we don't get bored, but they can move your story along. I often use *The Emotion Thesaurus* during dialogue. It helps me show the action tags better and in doing so, convey emotions or hints of them.

Try writing a brief dialogue while applying the things from today's lesson.

_____

_____

_____

_____

_____

_____

_____

_____

_____

_____

_____

_____

_____

_____

_____

_____

_____

_____

_____

"And He who sits on the throne said, 'Behold, I am making all things new.' And He said, 'Write, for these words are faithful and true'" (Revelation 21:5 NET).

When the Lord puts a message in our hearts to write, we receive the same command He gave John in Revelation 21:5. Would He give us a message to share, burn it into our subconscious until we obey and write, if He didn't mean us to share what He revealed?

Lesson 5 Homework:

1. Search for dialogue passages in your writing project. If you don't have any yet, write one or two.
2. Go back and determine where you might improve your dialogue.
3. What changes did you make? Bring examples to our next meeting.

Suggested Resources and Reading:

www.thepersonalities.com

www.livewritebreathe.com/talking-heads-syndrome/

www.nybookeditors.com/2018/02/dont-make-these-mistakes-when-writing-dialogue/

Silver Boxes by Florence Littauer (This has nothing to do with writing, but everything to do with words and their impact.)

Personality Plus by Florence Littauer

The Urban Thesaurus by Angela Ackerman & Becca Puglisi

The Rural Thesaurus by Angela Ackerman & Becca Puglisi

(These last two suggested books can help keep our talking heads grounded.)

The Sword and a Pen

12 Lessons for Christian Writers

"If a man is called to be a street sweeper, he should sweep streets even as a Michaelangelo painted, or Beethoven composed music or Shakespeare wrote poetry. He should sweep streets so well that all the hosts of heaven and earth will pause to say, 'Here lived a great street sweeper who did his job well.'" ~Martin Luther King, Jr.

"Mediocrity will never do. You are capable of something better." ~Gordon B. Hinckley

"I do the very best I know how, the very best I can, and I mean to keep on doing so until the end." ~Abraham Lincoln

Lesson 6—Editor's Pet Peeves

Focal verse for lesson 6: "But you are A CHOSEN RACE, A royal PRIESTHOOD, A HOLY NATION, A PEOPLE FOR God's OWN POSSESSION, so that you may proclaim the **excellencies** of Him who has called you out of darkness into His marvelous light;" (1 Peter 2:9 NAS95-emphasis mine).

"But you are the ones chosen by God, chosen for the high calling of priestly work, chosen to be a holy people, God's instruments to do his work and speak out for him, to tell others of the night-and-day difference he made for you—" (1 Peter 2:9 MSG).

Lesson 6 Introduction

While the word excellencies found in Peter's letter referred to moral excellency, it also translates to virtue. In a world where authors often write with less than moral excellence or virtuous skills, can we shine a light of excellence? In 1 Peter 2:12, the beloved apostle goes on to say, "Keep your behavior excellent among the Gentiles, so that in the thing in which they slander you as evildoers, they may because of your good deeds, as they observe them, glorify God in the day of visitation."

How does that speak to writers? For me, if I have a critic attack my books, articles, blogs, whatever, I don't want it to be from poor skills and habits. Hence the reason we gathered as a group — to learn a more excellent way. May we never have someone discount our work because we didn't give it our best. From the beginning, consider making it your goal to create writing that rivals the best. Although you may feel far from that goal, continue learning and practicing skills, regardless of what you read from "bestsellers."

See yourself as an artist and remember for whom you create your art of writing. Ultimately, we glorify God with our works of art. He chose us to write and speak His truths, always showing (not telling) the wondrous things He does because of our relationship with Him through Jesus.

What do you glean from these two verses in 1 Peter?

_____

_____

_____

_____

_____

_____

_____

_____

_____

_____

Homework?

In our last lesson, I challenged you to write and prepare to share a dialogue. How did that work for you? After last week's discussion, do you feel better equipped to write engaging dialogue?

_____

_____

_____

_____

_____

Did you ever wonder what makes an editor crazy? What makes them read a page or two of your writing and not want to continue? What causes a hired editor to charge extra money or reject your project altogether? And what potentially places your hard-fought manuscript in an acquisitions editor's dreaded slush pile?

Some of the material in this lesson may sound familiar, because we talked about it in previous lessons. Hopefully, it also seems familiar because you actively apply it to your writing now. Be sure to explore your questions about any of these areas as we dive in to editor's pet peeves.

Disclaimer: These areas come from years of experience in the world of magazines and both fiction and non-fiction book editing. While they may not encompass every possible pet peeve of all editors, they represent a good cross-section of potential trouble spots for writers and aspiring writers.

Expectations of Writers and Editors

Teachable Spirit

New Author vs. Seasoned Professional. Regardless of your level of expertise, keep your spirit teachable. Life requires continued learning. Remember, the writing industry changes constantly. As writers, we must read books, blogs, etc. to change with the times.

What worked over 100 years ago, 25 years ago, even five years ago may not apply today. While superb skills never fail, the way we present stories changes with the times. A book written long ago often includes long descriptive passages, some of which have nothing to do with the story. Don't believe me? When Victor Hugo wrote *Les Misérables* in 1862, he included a long passage about the war about one-third of the way into the book. Why? It had little to do with the tale, and for most of us reading today, it comes across as boring and unnecessary. Perhaps Hugo's original readers wanted these facts about the war. By the time we publish a book today, our readers already have every scrap of news available. They don't need us to give them details—unless the book comes from an insider's look at an event.

We must know what resonates with our readers. That said, we live in the world but not of it. Just because readers today don't necessarily have good grammar or recognize it doesn't give us an excuse to bail on improving ours. Up against not only other books but also against movies, television, social media, games, etc., we have the task of immediately pulling readers into our story world. Gone are days when long openings without action appear to readers. Tomorrow, next week, in a year or a decade, we may be back at Hugo's style.

The point? Know what's up in the writing industry. In the last 15 years, many things changed, and our publishing world looks vastly different from 20 years ago.

"Give instruction to a wise man and he will be still wiser, teach a righteous man and he will increase his learning." (Prov 9:9 NAS95).

An Editor's Job

At some time in the future, you should reach a point where you need a professional editor—especially true if you travel the independent publishing route. If you choose a traditional publishing route, you may still want an editor to help polish your manuscript before submitting it. In the coming lessons, we'll talk about what comes after you finish your manuscript and ways to support and improve your writing. An ongoing writing group creates a perfect means for feedback and encouragement long-term. Fellow writers, while helpful, do not replace a professional editor. The money you spend improves a book, but it can also help develop your skills as you apply what he or she corrects or suggests during your edit.

We'll talk more about editors in our next lesson, but for now, let's look at the four main types of editing. Each editor may use personal terminology, so be sure you clarify his or her definition.

Content/Development/Substantive: encompasses overall improvement.

Line Edits: unique edit that falls between copyediting and developmental editing in intensity.

Copy Editing: broad and deep edit reviews all aspects of the manuscript. Less deep than content, development, or line editing.

Proofreading: last step of editing before going to publication; looks for grammar, spelling, and typing errors. May include header and footer, chapter title style, etc.

Now that you better understand an editor's role with your writing project, let's get into the meat of this lesson.

Obvious Errors — Unedited MSS

Pay attention to basic rules of grammar — capitalization, italics, quotations, etc.

Would you take something to a group you didn't at least read through one last time? A worthy editor makes poor writing good, good writing great, great writing extraordinary. Learn to self-edit at a basic level or use software to catch mistakes. As an editor, I can perform a better edit if I don't have to deal with obvious errors such as missing commas, misspelled words, missing words, etc. Take time to at the least run a grammar and spellcheck. This also enables an editor to go deeper with your work and focus on making it better, not just grammatically correct. Plus, you learn rules by reviewing your work.

Overused Words

Use the find/replace functionality in MS Word to search for common overused words. Recent example: one manuscript had 1369 instances of the word "that," most of which I cut. As part of a proofread, the client only paid two cents a word, so it didn't affect his overall cost of the project. But he paid extra for something he could have cut himself. What are the most common overused words we don't need in manuscripts? That, just, so, well, doubled words (and so, and yet, his own, etc.), and any other word you use repeatedly. If you think you repeat the same word, check.

In a content edit at \$.04/word, 3500 uses of "that" = \$140 + 2000 uses of "just" = \$80 + 500 times you use "so" = \$20 — a total of \$240 saved by taking time to review your work and remove extraneous words. These words may not bother a normal reader, but they drive an editor bonkers.

Repeated Words

The same word appearing multiple times in one sentence or paragraph and often throughout the MSS requires attention from the editor. While he or she may not change, the editor will at least notate the need for a synonym. Because editing often doesn't occur at one sitting, she probably will note the overuse numerous times. This also can become a distraction to an editor, keeping him or her from honing in on deeper improvements. Watch for these in writing and search for them before submitting a piece for editing or publication.

Passive Voice

While this may not bother many editors or readers, we can do better. Since we already spent time on passive verbs, this should serve as a point of review. As a reminder, what is a passive verb?

- A sentence where the subject is acted upon by the noun.
- A noun that acts on the subject after the fact.

Why avoid passive verbs?

- Slows reading—physiological effect happens in the brain.
- Boring and somewhat lazy writing.
- Often vague, can confuse readers.

Enough said? Any questions?

Auxiliary Verbs

A lesser-known term, auxiliary verbs appear often in writing. Like the passive verb, we don't see these as incorrect, but like overused words, do we need them? What is an auxiliary verb, anyway? An unnecessary word used with a verb. Consider the example below.

Example: She had talked with the principal.

Better: She talked with the principal.

Because the action happened in the past, why do we need had? We don't. It happened. Done.

Another example: He was watching television instead of writing.

Better: He watched television instead of writing.

These feel almost like a passive verb, but in this instance, "was" becomes an auxiliary verb. Again, unneeded.

Why avoid auxiliary verbs?

- Extraneous word which serves no purpose.
- Changes the meaning. Has talked indicates a continuous process. Unless you mean to convey something that commenced in the past and continues to the present, leave out has.

Telling Everything

We spent time with show, don't tell. Hopefully, you understand those concepts. If not, let's discuss it. While we can go into this again, we won't. Go back to lesson four and review if necessary. We can't show every scene, although the best books tell little and show most of the story. Even in telling, use an air of showing.

When writing, search for scenes that feel somewhat flat. Look for passives and filters (I saw, she understood, he remembered). These flags indicate telling over showing. Use all five senses in your writing—of course, not all at the same time. Express emotions instead of telling.

Along these same lines, let your emotions shine. I have yet to tell a writer to pull back emotions. We tend to hold back those raw, gut-clenching feelings. Release them on paper. Your writing friends, critique groups or partners, beta readers, someone will mention it if you go too far. Not likely.

Improper Dialogue Format

Last week, we discussed dialogue. Poorly formatted dialogue suggests an amateur writer. Whether good or bad, use the correct basic formatting. Yes, someone may correct it before publication, but it can make the speaker unclear and confuse an editor or anyone reading your MSS. And if no one corrects it, you have a reader who doesn't prefer you over another author.

Watch tags, too. Use what you need, keep them simple, and trying active tags sometimes instead of the boring he said, she said. Don't overuse your tags and watch for talking heads.

Other Potential Issues for Editors

Bible Stuff

Always capitalize Bible, the Word, Word of God, etc. This isn't negotiable. Do not, however, capitalize the words "biblical" or "godly."

While some publishers don't capitalize pronouns for God, Jesus, or Holy Spirit, many still do. I think He deserves capitalization. Err on the side of capitalization, but above all, retain consistency. If you capitalize half of the God pronouns, the editor must then decide your preference. Don't saddle him or her with that burden. Go one way or the other, but do it 100% of the time.

When using biblical references, which version did you use? If you leave this piece out, someone must either come back and ask you or try to guess — a game which may prove incorrect. What are the rules around biblical references?

Instead of using footnotes or endnotes to cite a Bible verse or passage, the correct versions used must appear on the copyright page. (Read the copyright permission in the front of your Bible. It states this clearly.)

When using only one version, the verbiage on the copyright page denotes this. At the first quote, show the abbreviated version. Example: MSG=The Message. All other quotations do not need the abbreviated reference.

If you use multiple versions of the Bible, list each on the copyright page and mark every verse with the appropriate abbreviation. (KJV, NIV, NAS95, NASB, ESV, etc.)

The format for quotations varies, and neither APA nor CMOS style guides address this adequately. Generally, set off the quote with double quotation marks. For any quotation within the verse, use a single quotation mark. At the end of the quotation, include the reference within parentheses. Punctuation at the end of the quote is questionable, but the period after the closing parenthesis is not.

Again, inconsistency and excluding the version create the biggest headaches for an editor. And if submitting to a publisher, they might not throw you on the slush pile, but then they might. Work toward better than average and use the correct formatting.

Example: "Jesus said, 'I am the way, the truth, and the life. No one comes to the Father but by me.'" (John 14:6 KJV).

If you have a long passage and choose to offset it with hanging indents, you may want to italicize the entire passage, but you don't need the outer quotations marks in this instance. The offset shows a quote. Use normal dialogue markings and don't forget the reference and version at the end.

Proper footnotes and citations

In an e-book, a hyperlink to a citation creates a beautiful interactive feature. However, this doesn't work in print. Seriously. Try using your finger to click a link from a print book. Nothing happens. Maybe one day — not today. Unless you insert a QR Code instead of the written link. Now that's a way to make your print book interactive. I digress.

We see little of this in fiction, but you might use endnotes if your fictional book warrants references. At the very least, you might include a reference page at the end of the book. Nonfiction, though, often uses quoted material or referenced statistics, etc. In these cases, be sure to use footnotes or endnotes alongside proper citations. While an editor may add these for you, don't expect it.

Refer to the document at www.texasradicalwriters.com (see suggested reading at the end of this lesson) if you need help with using MS Word technology. Let the software do the work for you, then you don't have to worry about whether you did it correctly. You can also use the software to create a bibliography or reference page with the click of a button.

When you quote from a book, article, web document, etc., neglecting to cite the source might create issues with copyright or plagiarism. The Fair Use Act allows a reasonable amount of content quotation, but it also requires acknowledging the original creator.

Lesson 6 Homework:

1. Using the find option in MS Word, look in your manuscript for the number of times you use the words that, so, just, well, and any other words you might overuse. Where possible, delete the extraneous words.
2. Search for places where you used passive verbs and change them into active sentences.

3. Look for places where you used auxiliary verbs. Unless they alter the meaning of your sentence, remove them.
4. If you use Bible verses in your work, check to make sure you properly formatted them.
5. Play with the MS Word functionality for adding footnotes or endnotes, citations, creating a bibliography and creating an automatic table of contents.

Suggested reading:

Bird by Bird by Anne Lamont

Self-editing for Fiction Writers by Renni Browne and Dave King

https://writer.com/blog/a-live-grammar-checklist-the-most-common-grammar-mistakes/

https://prowritingaid.com/grammatical-errors

The Sword and a Pen

12 Lessons for Christian Writers

"I'm writing a first draft and reminding myself that I'm simply shoveling sand into a box so that later I can build castles." ~Shannon Hale

"Dream with your heart. Write with your soul. But edit with your head." ~Jennifer Spredemann

Lesson 7—Draft Done. Now What?

Focal verses for lesson 7: "Take hold of instruction; do not let go. Guard her, for she is your life." (Proverbs 4:13 NAS95).

"Heed instruction and be wise, and do not neglect it." (Proverbs 8:33 NAS95)

Lesson 7 Introduction

The book of Proverbs contains many references to instruction, as do many other verses in the Bible. No matter how long we write, we can always use improvement in our work. The input of other experienced writers and professional editors can take our work from mediocre to outstanding, from good to great, and from ordinary to extraordinary.

Those who don't despise instruction grow in skills. Learning from others gives us perspectives we may never see without the feedback. Always be open to learning more about writing, but use discernment for the source.

You can perform a great deal of self-editing and should. As we talked about in lesson six, the most frustrating moment for an editor arrives with an unedited manuscript. After you finish writing that first draft, take time to revisit your work and make corrections.

During the past six weeks, we looked at planning a book and starting the process. We visited some mechanics of writing well, and we discussed pet peeves for not only editors but also for those who read when common mistakes appear in a published book.

While you made progress on your book, a finished draft doesn't often happen unless you spent quality, focused time writing. Realistically, life interrupts our writing. However, eventually, you will finish that first draft.

Last week, we ventured into the world of perfectionism. In *The Artist's Way*, Julia Cameron spoke to the idea of perfectionism.

> *Perfectionism has nothing to do with getting it right. It has nothing to do with fixing things. It has nothing to do with standards. Perfectionism is a refusal to let yourself move ahead. It is a loop — an obsessive, debilitating closed system that causes you to get stuck in the details of what you are writing or painting or making and to lose sight of the whole. Instead of creating freely and allowing errors to reveal themselves later as insights, we often get mired in getting the details right. We correct our originality into a uniformity that lacks passion and spontaneity. "Do not fear mistakes," Miles Davis told us. "There are none."* [7]

I love this reminder. While we strive for excellence, we cannot become so entrenched in the editing process we never finish the first draft. Write, finish, and then we can move on to the next steps with moving your manuscript to the finished book. And what are those next steps? Stay tuned, because we're going there next.

Celebrate!

Yes, you read (heard) that correctly. You finished writing the first draft. No matter how long or short of a time it took, you accomplished something not everyone does. How big of a celebration? I suppose that depends on what you wrote. An article or short story might be as simple as taking a coffee break. A book — go out to dinner. Make this a momentous occasion. A first draft required sacrifices, concentration, and hours of work. Don't take it lightly. But remember, you still have work. Your "baby" needs time to develop a bit more.

Take a minute to plan a small celebration for the day you complete the first draft of your book. How will you celebrate?

---

[7] (Cameron 1992, 2002)

_____

_____

_____

_____

_____

_____

_____

_____

_____

Marinate

After finishing your final draft, let it rest. Many authors term this period as marinating time. If you begin an editing process immediately after finishing a writing project, you face multiple things.

Physical, mental, and perhaps emotional or spiritual fatigue follow the let down of the final words of a manuscript. Give yourself time to rest. Trust me, you will still think about the manuscript during this time, but try to forget it. Allowing yourself this break provides the ability to come back and attack the remaining steps with fresh energy. If you don't take this time, the next step feels much more like a chore than a pleasure.

Stepping back gives you perspective and better prepares you to forge ahead. If thoughts about your work surface during this time, do nothing with them. If necessary, jot down notes for the next phase — things you want to add, scenes you want to reword or look at again. During this break, you may realize you left out something important. Again, jot it down, knowing you can add it after the break.

How long do you let a manuscript marinate? It all depends... For shorter pieces, you may only need to let it rest overnight. For novels, novellas, a collection of short stories or essays, let it rest a minimum of two weeks — especially if you pushed hard to finish the manuscript. James Scott Bell suggests two weeks with three as better, four weeks if possible.

Some manuscripts marinate for months. If needed, go for it. I suspect you won't wait too long because after all the work of writing, you can't wait to get back to it. Perhaps work on another project during this time off or read books on the craft of writing. But be certain you have a plan in place for returning to the work and finishing what you started.

In the same way God sometimes gives us time to prepare for the next phase of our lives, give yourself time to prepare for the next phases of finishing the writing process. Set a tentative date for returning to the project, and set your mind on completing what the Lord began with you.

Self-Editing

After an adequate time of marination, return to your project. Go back to the previous lessons and read through them again if needed. Prepare to polish your work. This process can take a few days or months. Press on and finish the race with confidence and assurance in making your book the best you can.

Over the next three or four days, read through your manuscript without making extensive corrections. Some people prefer printing the entire thing; others do it online. You might have your computer read it to you. (Hint: that option appears on your Review tab in MS Word.) The first read-through helps confirm your structure and flow.

During the first pass, note any scenes that feel flat. Watch for passive verbs and mark them. You can correct spelling and grammar when you see it, but don't focus as much on those parts of the self-edit during this first reading. If you discover repetitive or overused words, highlight them or create a note. If working online, the "New Comment" on the review tab provides an opportunity to make a quick note for yourself. You can also use Track Changes if you want to see what you changed. Save any changes with a new file name so you can always go back to the previous file if you accidentally change or remove something. It happens.

After reading the entire manuscript, correct any repetitive words. Using find and replace functionality makes deleting overused words quick and easy. Go back to the repeated words with a thesaurus in hand. Correct those.

Third, work through the manuscript and revisit the scenes that felt lackluster. Apply what you learned during our study or in reading and make those scenes sparkle. If you get bored writing or reading your work, so will the end reader. If scenes make little impact on the overall story, consider cutting them. Take as much time as you need to finish this part of a self-edit.

You can repeat these steps, and many authors do. Few writers walk away satisfied with only one editing session. If you used track changes, go back and review every change, accepting or rejecting them. This also allows you another reading of the manuscript to find things you might have previously missed.

Finally, use software to help you seek and destroy grammatical and spelling errors. No matter how well we write or edit, we all miss something. At the very least, run a grammar and spellcheck. You may want one last read-through or share with another writer or friend who will give you honest feedback.

When satisfied with your edits, move forward.

How do you feel about editing, revisions and rewrites?

_____

_____

_____

_____

_____

_____

_____

_____

_____

_____

Consider Professional Editing

Not everyone hires a professional editor, but perhaps we all should. Unfortunately, editors cost money you may not have to spend. Understandable. However, an experienced editor adds value to your book and can take it to a higher level. Today's options for self-publishing means many authors skip this step and put a less-than-best product on the market. If you want to hire an editor but can't afford one, approach one with honesty. Consider the following options.

- Barter. If you have skills to help an editor, he or she may provide an edit in exchange for your assistance in other areas.

- Request a deep assessment of your work or a critique of a specified number of pages. Take what the editor provides and apply it to your manuscript.
- Ask for an edit of the first 50 pages… or 100… or as many as you can afford. Generally, the way you write in the first pages continues for the book's remainder. By paying for fewer pages, you receive feedback and can apply what you learned from a good edit.

Before approaching an editor, know what type of edit you require. Not only does that help the editor provide an accurate cost estimate, but it establishes expectations for both sides. As the author, you have the final say on the way you write your book. Although an editor has experience, knowledge, and objectivity, she or he may not fully understand your heart. The final decision to accept or reject an editor's changes lives with the author. Consider the recommendations, but never let an editor take over your work. The best editors strive to maintain your voice when rewording anything or suggesting changes.

The section below explains various types of edits with a price range (subject to change). All editors use personal terminology preferences and set individual prices. Make sure to ask what an editor includes in a specific edit. Many editors provide a low-cost assessment to determine the best edit for you. If you're comfortable with your manuscript, you many need only a copyedit or proofread.

Remember that adage, "You get what you pay for?" Hiring a low-cost editor doesn't always mean you get the best edit for your money. Ask questions of a prospective editor and don't fear asking for references. With better editors, you many need to wait for their schedule to clear. Consider contracting with an editor when you begin the self-edit phase of your project.

Editing definitions

Editorial Assessment: Also known as a manuscript evaluation, the assessment provides an overall review of your work and often comes with a recommendation for further editing. This edit can equip you with overall improvements, but doesn't provide specifics beyond a few examples.

Expectations:
- High-level suggestions for improvement
- Editor's Overall Opinion
- Strengths & weaknesses
    - In plot
    - Characters
    - Dialog
    - Structure
    - other
- Summary without rewrites or correction
- $46-$70/hour or $.03-$.07/word

Book Doctoring: Some editors may use the term developmental for this type of edit. If you have a well-written manuscript, or you're willing to learn and improve, you won't need anything this deep. Book doctoring works best for those who have a story but don't write well. A sub-service of ghostwriting, book doctoring enhances and develops a manuscript on behalf of an author.

Expectations:
- Developmental editing tasks
- Rewrite and/or restructure passages from the manuscript
- Similar to ghostwriting, but enhances the author's work rather than writing from scratch
- $61-70/hour or $.06-$.07/word

Content/Development/Substantive: Many manuscripts need this level of editing which encompasses overall improvement. This level of editing considers a work's organization and presentation. It involves tightening and clarifying at a chapter, scene, paragraph, and sentence level. It may include grammar and style, although the editor won't focus on these elements as much. From an editor's perspective, self-edit your grammar so the one you hire can better focus on content.

Since many editors consider development an offshoot of ghostwriting, adding content where needed or rounding out a skeleton manuscript, be sure to clarify what an editor means by "development." If an editor says you need a development edit, be sure to clarify his or her meaning.

Expectations:

- Summary—similar to assessment
- Specific suggestions but doesn't rewrite passages
- May recommend reorganizing
- Proposes solutions
- Some line or copy edits to teach changes to the author
- $46-$70/hour or $.03-$.07/word

Line Edits: This refers to a unique edit that falls between copyediting and developmental editing in intensity. In line editing, the editor looks at your book line by line or at the paragraph level and analyzes each sentence, considering word choice and the power and meaning of a sentence. The editor considers syntax and whether a sentence needs tightening. Line editing helps makes your prose sing.

The highest level of editing, except for book doctoring, line editing also costs the most.

Expectations:

- Corrections of errors
- Focus on language and style
- Not intent on catching every grammar or spelling error
- $46-50/hour or $.04 to $.05/word

Copy Editing: This broad and deep edit reviews all aspects of the manuscript, including but not limited to grammar and style. Less deep than content, development, or line editing, this common level catches many mistakes an author misses. Most editors offer something between a proofread and content at this level. This may also include verification of biblical references, but be sure and confirm if you need it, as this may incur an extra cost.

Expectations:

- Correct spelling, grammar, usage and punctuation
- Check cross-references
- Perfect wording and overall flow

- Consistency and accuracy across the manuscript, plus overall final review
- $36-50/hour or $.02-$.05/word

Proofreading: The last step of editing before going to publication, this edit looks for common errors, spelling, grammatical mistakes, etc. The best proofread happens after formatting and before final publication. That way, your proofreader can also assess the layout. Many times, editors receive a manuscript for proofreading prior to formatting. In that case, they may still look at headers and footers, chapter title style, etc.

A last check for typos and other errors, every completed manuscript needs this edit. While an author may opt to take on this editing role, it never hurts to have a second pair of eyes. An author often completes this edit (alone or with beta readers) from a digital or print proof copy.

Expectations:
- Check for spelling and typographical errors
- Check style for chapter titles
- Check headers, footers, flow, etc.
- Check overall look of manuscript, flow for print and/or e-book
$31-$45/hour or $.02-$.05

Last thoughts of the editing phase of a book. Some editors combine types and price the project accordingly. Be sure to understand what an editor provides when hiring one. Editors are human, and the best ones may miss something. Even a proofread can leave a mistake. As the author, you have the final responsibility for checking a proof copy of your book — regardless of the publishing route you choose. Expect to find one or more errors in a printed proof copy — and marvel if you don't.

To find an editor, get references from other writers. You can also attend workshops and conferences. Visit legitimate websites, but be cautious. Just because someone says they're an editor doesn't mean they know anything about writing or the industry.   Please see the resources area for some recommendations of websites to use. Don't expect to fall next in line on an editor's busy schedule. Patience, a fruit of the spirit, is a virtue. But be careful about praying for patience. The answer may involve events you don't want to face.

Be sure to match your style with the editor. A western writer turned editor may not fit your story. One who edits only nonfiction may not fit your latest novel, and a fiction only editor may know nothing about nonfiction. Ask questions, request references or a sample edit, and seek discernment from Holy Spirit. He already knows exactly who He plans to work with you, so pray for direction. Sometimes, He may lead you to an editor who needs exactly what you wrote.

After all the editing, celebrate again, because you are one step closer to the finish line.

If you had to choose an edit at this point, which do you think you'll need? If a professional edit isn't an option, how will you improve your manuscript prior to publication?

_____

_____

_____

_____

_____

_____

_____

Consider Publishing Options and decide

In the next lesson, we'll dive into details about publishing options, the pros and cons of each, and what each option requires of the author. But at this point in your process, you must decide which route you plan to take. Good time for prayer concerning this step and following the way the Lord leads you. Remain open to His answer for everything you write.

Word of caution here. When you look at publishers, be super cautious. Conduct diligent research and never sign a contract without a microscopic review. A contract without a termination clause means RUN. I repeat this caution often. Predators love those with a story who simply want to share it. They seek new authors who don't know the industry. Pray over every opportunity, seeking discernment along the way.

You basically have three options for publishing, and within those options a few sub-options. Within traditional publishing, you can opt for a larger house (publisher) in Christian or secular publishing, which often requires an agent. Smaller traditional publishers may not require an agent, although some agents may choose a smaller house to publish your book.

Although an option, I don't recommend vanity press. Many of these companies market themselves as traditional publishers or as self-publishers. They charge exorbitant prices for services. Some charge nothing up front, which makes them look like a traditional publisher. But they usually market primarily to the author and make money on the backend with promotion and overpriced books. When promoted as a self-publisher, they charge exorbitant prices for services and price books higher than normal.

Self-publishing, or indie publishing, also has sub-options. You first need to know what POD (print on demand) platforms exist and the nuances of various ones. Experience from an editor or other writers can help in this area. You can pay someone for services to prepare your book for publication, although, if you have technical skills, you may choose to save money doing this yourself. Beware of those who overcharge for publishing assistance. More on this next week. If you opt to do the work yourself, consider paying a consultation fee for an experienced author to help you through the process. Some editors also provide this service.

Do you have a sense of how you will pursue publication? Which one?

_____

_____

_____

_____

Create a Marketing Plan

If you traditionally publish a book, the publisher expects to see a marketing plan as a part of your submission. Equally or more important for an independent author, you need an idea of how to market your book. Make this a part of your process and work on it during the down times from writing. We go into more detail in Week Nine, so I won't bog you down here. Keep in mind, it's best to do this before you finish publishing.

While a traditional publisher expects a completed plan, preparation can include brainstorming ideas, researching, or creating a simple list of ideas for marketing—the where and how of it. You can always plan on hiring a publicist or someone to create materials for you, or even paying for a marketing package.

Watch for homework on this one.

Assemble Beta Readers and a Launch Team

At any time while working on your book, jot down people you trust to read your book before anyone else can. Consider about ten readers for this task, asking them to provide honest feedback, alert you of any missed errors, and write a brief review after reading. Select people who support and encourage you and will recommend your book to others. As an option, if you have a well-known contact or one with established credibility, request an endorsement. Reward this team with acknowledgment in the book and perhaps an autographed copy for their personal library.

Not every author hosts a book launch, and some choose to do an online version. Consider whether you want to throw a big celebration, and if so, plan for it ahead of your expected release date.

Proofread Your Book and Publish

Regardless of how you publish your book, obtain a printed copy and read it from cover to cover. That includes both covers. Take this step seriously as your last time to discover any missed errors. Then, breathe deep, approve the galley copies, and publish the book. Congratulations. You are a published author.

Celebrate and market that baby.

Birthing a child calls for celebration. Then come the sleepless nights with a newborn and years of changing diapers, feeding, clothing, dealing with everyday life.

In the same way, a book baby requires attention after the release day. People can't read your book if they don't know it exists. Hopefully, those closest to you get to celebrate with you and tell everyone they know about your book. The number you sell and lives you touch depends directly on how well you market it—alongside God's grace. You may be in the middle of the next book at this point, but you can't forget to let people know about the previous one. More to come.

Don't gloss over the release of your book. You should celebrate in some way—even if that means a quiet dinner out or standing on the porch thanking God for His direction throughout the entire process.

Congratulations on finishing your book and walking in obedience to the promptings of the Holy Spirit. Well done, good and faithful servant.

What is your idea of the best celebration for completing your book?

_____

_____

_____

_____

_____

_____

_____

_____

_____

_____

Lesson 7 Homework:

1. Continue working on your manuscript.
2. Research and brainstorm marketing ideas. (See resources suggested sites.) Be prepared to share a few ideas next week.
3. Consider potential beta readers (two or three) and a launch team (about ten). Compile a list (ongoing process) of those you may invite to fill these roles.

Suggested Resources:

Self-Editing for Fiction Writers: How to edit yourself into print by Renni Browne and Dave King

Revision & Self-Editing: Techniques for transforming your first draft into a finished novel by James Scott Bell

www.roaringlambs.org/book-marketing1 This site offers reasonable prices for a marketing plan, but it also provides an idea of what you might include on a personal plan.

www.authormedia.com This site offers blogs and podcasts ripe with book marketing suggestions, among many other interesting topics for writers.

www.kindlepreneur.com Another site for writers that includes more than you can imagine, but also has many ideas for marketing.

The Sword and a Pen
12 Lessons for Christian Writers

"Confidence is going after Moby Dick in a rowboat and taking the tartar sauce with you." ~Zig Ziglar

"Publication is a marathon, not a sprint. Writing the book is only the start." ~Jo Linsdell

"Turning a manuscript into a book is easy; getting the manuscript ready to become a book is hard." ~A.P. Fuchs

Lesson 8—Publishing Options

Focal verse for lesson 8: "I pray with great faith for you, because I'm fully convinced that the One who began this glorious work in you will faithfully continue the process of maturing you and will put his finishing touches to it until the unveiling of our Lord Jesus Christ!" (Philippians 1:6 TPT).

Lesson 8 Introduction

Publishing anything creates a sense of wonder in the life of a writer. If someone publishes a piece you wrote—be it an article, devotional, poetry, book, or whatever—it enhances your credibility. But don't let someone else determine your value. If God called you to write one thing or for the rest of your life, you are a writer.

Say it out loud. *I am a writer!*

Do you realize if you post something original on Facebook or write a blog on a website you have published your words? You are published. Think about it. You have something online other people can read, reflect on, comment to. Scary? Maybe a bit when we consider that most of us think little before putting something online for the world to see. Don't let that intimidate you.

Go back to why you write. God began this journey with you, and He won't stop. Now's the time for reflection on your why and to press in over what He wants you to do with what you wrote. If you write a book, the next obvious step (after all the editing, revisions, etc.) progresses to making it available through publication.

Published books go back to ancient worlds, written on clay tablets and papyrus. With the printing press invented in the mid-1400s, the number of printed books grew exponentially, making them available to millions of readers. It changed the world and introduced publishers, who accepted the financial risk of creating books, hoping to sell enough copies to cover what they spent.

In today's world, traditional publish remains the avenue many writers choose to create a book from a manuscript. Even 15-20 years ago, people looked down on those who personally published books. In recent years, though, independent (or self) publishing gained ground as a viable option. Some traditionally published authors may still sniff at a self-published author, but those who read the books don't care as much about who published the book as about how well they like it, whether the author wrote well and gave them something memorable, and how the book left them feeling.

Which publishing option works best? It depends on the writer. With so many options available, choosing one gets more difficult all the time, and unfortunately, the industry has many predators who take advantage of unsuspecting authors. Jesus said, "Behold, I send you out as sheep in the midst of wolves; so be shrewd as serpents and innocent as doves." (Matthew 10:16 NAS95).

If you remember nothing else from this course, pay attention to this warning. Seek wisdom before signing a contract with any company, and running it by an attorney never hurts if you aren't sure what you're signing. This holds true for agents, editors, and publishers. With that warning in mind, let's look at publishing options.

As stated last week, you have basically three options: traditional, vanity press, and self-publishing (AKA independent publishing). I list vanity press, although I seldom recommend using this option. Vanity press may also present themselves as traditional or self-publishers, but they cost a lot of money—thus, not your best option. We'll go over as much as possible during this lesson, but most of the "how-to" is something for later. I will strive to give you as many resources as possible to guide you in making this decision.

Traditional Publishing

Traditional publishers produce books without cost to the author. They accept all financial risks, assume copyright for the term of a contract, control and create interior layout and content, finalize titles, and create the cover. They print books in selected formats and may or may not request additional rights for e-books, movies, etc. The ISBN (international standard book number) also belongs to the publisher.

Per Merriam-Webster, publishing is the business or profession of the commercial production and issuance of literature, information, musical scores or sometimes recordings, or art. A traditional publisher may offer an advance against royalties, based on the volume they believe an author will sell. Once royalties rise above that advance amount, then they send checks for additional royalties. They do not accept all manuscripts for publication.

Now that you know what we mean by traditional publishing, how do you determine if this is the right path for you? Who are the traditional publishers today, and how do you choose one?

The top five publishers (as of 11/1/2023) include Penguin Random House, Hachette Livre, HarperCollins, Simon and Shuster, and Macmillan Publishers. HarperCollins now owns Zondervan and Thomas Nelson. I won't go into the details of all the publishers, but encourage you to read Steve Laube's post titled "Who Owns Whom in Publishing." (See link in the suggested resources.)

Reality check. Unless you meet an acquisitions editor for one of these companies at a conference, you need an agent for them to consider your book. Harsh reality, but that's today's writing world. Many of the smaller publishers, Baker, Barbour, Charisma House, Harvest House, Tyndale House, etc. may or may not require an agent. But these are true traditional publishers.

You may want to invest $9.99 in an annual online subscription to *The Christian Writers Guide* for a full list of publishers for not only books but also magazines, writing courses and more. Regardless, always check a publisher's website to determine the type of books they publish and their guidelines for submissions.

Pros of Traditional Publishing

Provide work at no cost to the author

Formatting interior, cover design, some editing and marketing, etc.

Provide ISBN

Have established marketing channels and relationships

Have sales representatives and marketing people on staff

Industry recognition

Assistance with marketing — press releases, potential materials and advertising

Note: the author retains responsibility for marketing the book

Experience in the industry

Aim for high quality

Cons of Traditional Publishing

Must submit a query letter, proposal, or both

May require an agent, which takes 15% of royalties on average

Royalties normally range from 8 to 10% (exceptions to the rule)

Assume copyright for term of contract

Choose title and cover — may or may not accept suggestions

Control content — may insist on extensive removal or editing

Layout control — don't always listen to authors' desires

No guarantee of book placement in book or retail stores

Difficult for new authors without big platforms, especially for non-fiction

Control of retail prices

Long lead time — not on your timetable

Explanation of Royalties

Net Price X royalty% = author payout

Net Price = what the publisher receives from selling books to book dealers (generally 40-60% of retail price)

Example: $20 retail with a 50% wholesale discount; $10.00 net X 10% = $1.00/book. If agented, which many large publishers require, 15% of that $1.00 goes to the agent, leaving the author with $0.85/book sold. *(Note: if you receive an advance for your book, you won't get any additional royalties until they surpass the amount of your advance.)*

Myths of Traditional Publishing

If traditionally published, your book will automatically be carried by Barnes and Nobles, Walmart, Target and every other probable place you can imagine.

The publisher will take care of all marketing for you. All you need to do is sit back, relax, and collect your royalties.

You'll get rich from publishing your first book

You can quit your day job, because they'll have another advance for the rest of your series and any other books you write.

You'll be a bestseller in no time.

Tips for Traditional Publishing

Do your homework

Know the publisher—what they publish, guidelines for submission, whether they require an agent, query, online proposal, etc.

Have your manuscript critiqued and/or edited prior to submission

Create a market plan to increase the likelihood of acceptance

Never assume because a company says they're a traditional publisher it is true. Watch for red flags.

- High priced books
- Requirement to pay them for anything. True traditional publishers do not ask authors to pay them. They pay a small royalty to the author.
- Complaints with BBB, online or in the news

Final Thoughts on Traditional Publishing

Publishers have been around for centuries, and yes, they know the industry well. For some people, this route works extremely well. In some ways, they changed with the times. In others, not so much. Landing a contract with a publisher doesn't mean they will pick up your next book, although they may love working with you and want everything you write. It can go either way, and if you choose this path, you'll need to understand how to create queries and proposals. Regardless of your path, you need a marketing plan, so don't be afraid to learn about and create one.

Prepare mentally and emotionally for rejections with this path. The best writers of all time received many rejections before ever getting a contract with a traditional publisher. Persevere and plan on submitting to multiple publishers.

In the space below, record any questions you have about traditional publishing that we might not have covered.

_____

_____

_____

_____

_____

_____

_____

_____

_____

_____

_____

Vanity Press Publishing

Vanity Press Publishing is the business of producing books at a cost to the author. They accept virtually all manuscripts if the author will pay them. While they normally take care of all the work (interior layout, formatting, book cover design, etc.), the author pays for their services — typically thousands of dollars. With Vanity Press, an author usually maintains copyright and may have input on the way a book looks. They may have more control over retail pricing, content, and title as well as how the cover looks. In most cases, the cost includes author copies (may require purchasing many books as part of their package). They may provide royalties if people buy from their website. They may also include distribution and an ISBN on behalf of the author.

*Many of these publishers call themselves "traditional" publishers, producing books at no cost, but then they require a large purchase of the printed copies at a "wholesale" price or payment for "extra" services. Or they may control the price of the book and market primarily to the authors.

With the increased popularity of self-publishing, some vanity presses now market themselves as "self-publishers," but in truth, they are vanity press. Beware when searching publishers.

Vanity Press Publishing Pros

(Note: if working with a vanity press company, clarify these points and make sure if and to what level they provide all services.)

Provide all work (formatting interior, cover design, editing, and marketing, etc.)

Provide ISBN (usually as part of the package price — confirm)

Have established marketing channels and relationships

Have sales representatives and marketing people on staff

Industry recognition

Assistance with marketing — press releases, potential materials and advertising (author retains responsibility for marketing the book)

Experience in the industry

Tend toward high quality to remain competitive

Shorter lead time than traditional

Vanity Press Publishing Cons

Tend toward high cost

May offer larger royalties, but don't sell many books except to the author

Most likely use templates for covers, so designs aren't always unique

Sub-contract work to the lowest bidder — may not maintain high quality

Add-on costs possible

"Print cost" of books may include their cost plus a markup

May follow traditional methods of large print runs or use POD (verify)

Takes about 3-9 months depending on the company

Royalty rates vary by company; know how they compute royalties.

Myths of Vanity Press Publishing

Full edits come with the package cost

They'll market your book well

You have wider distribution than with self-publishing

You'll recover the costs of publishing

It is the only way to get a quality book published other than traditional

Tips for Vanity Press Publishing

Do your homework—be extremely careful (use provided website resources, online complaints, BBB, etc.)

Know the publisher—what they publish, their guidelines for submission, what exactly you get for the money, etc.

If the contract has no termination clause, RUN away

Make sure the contract outlines all details and costs

Have your book professionally edited — they may include editing in the package, but it usually includes only proofreading

Create a market plan for your use

Final Thoughts on Vanity Press Publishing

I never enjoy seeing an author spend over $10,000 to publish their book, especially because you have less expensive options. However, for some people, this feels like a better option. If you choose this path, stick with legitimate, well-known publishers (Xulon, Xilibris, Abbott Press) or others with excellent reputations. Fully understand what they provide for the money. If the "package" includes editing, ask which kind of edit they provide. If they include marketing, ask what exactly that entails.

Pray for discernment during the initial discussions and listen intently to what Holy Spirit tells you. Do not let a high-pressure sales representative talk you into signing quickly. Review the contract closely. If anything smells fishy, say thank you and discontinue negotiations with that company. Don't be afraid to back down.

Do you have any questions about Vanity Press Publishing?

_____

_____

_____

_____

_____

_____

_____

_____

_____

_____

Independent Publishing

When an author decides to create and print their book, they can choose from self-publishing or POD (print on demand). With Independent Publishing, an author takes all financial risks, pays for services or does the work themselves, decides how to distribute the finished product and must also produce all marketing materials or pay someone for the service. With this option, the author retains copyright, controls content, cover design, pricing and all other facets.

*As with all publishing, beware of predators and scam artists. They abound in this choice.

Independent Publishing Options

True self-publishing: the author does all the work (or pays for the services) and then takes the final product to a physical print company. This option is very labor-intensive and high cost, plus it does not include distribution, ISBN, or any marketing. This option is not recommended unless you know a great deal about the industry.

POD (print on demand): facilitated by companies, the author still does most of the work (or pays for services). However, legitimate companies offer assistance and online tools as well as distribution and other options. The cost can be minimal if you can do most or all the work. Most independent publishers use this route.

Independent Publishing Pros

Total control — pricing, cover, title, content, copyright, etc.

Author copies of book are usually lower cost

Typically higher royalties

E-book production is also easily available

High quality is possible

No rejections

Timetable on your terms

Faster turnaround than with traditional or vanity press

Expanded distribution available

Online tools, possible assistance, and community forums

Independent Publishing Cons

Author must do all the work or pay for services

Author must understand legalities and industry

Quality is only as good as the author makes it—little review

Having only self-imposed deadlines can delay publication

Author has full responsibility for marketing, including materials and implementation of plans

May have problems getting it into some retail outlets

Myths of Independent Publishing

You can't self-publish without spending a fortune.

You're a lousy writer, so this was the only way you could get published.

You will never be published traditionally if you self-publish.

You can't get your book in any bookstore if it's self-published.

Self-published authors aren't successful.

Self-publishing will make you wealthy.

It's okay if I just throw a book out there, even if it's poorly written and full of errors.

You must hire a graphic artist to format your book and design your cover.

Gutters don't matter. *(Note: Gutters refer to the inner space that prevents words from hiding or bumping against the binding.)*

Explanation of Royalties

While each POD offers various royalty percentages for print and e-book, the basics are the same. Based on your retail price, when a book sales, they deduct print or delivery costs, then pay a percent of the difference in royalties.

Example: Retail $15; print cost $5; X royalty of 35% =$3.50 royalty per book.

Tips for Independent Publishing

BEWARE of scammers

Have manuscript professionally edited (also helps with legalities)

Complete multiple self-edits

Always purchase a printed proof copy (unless it's an e-book only)

Prepare and follow a marketing plan

Use available tools and get or pay for services if necessary

Avoid using the POD company's stock photos and covers

Take advantage of someone else's expertise

Set deadlines and have someone hold you accountable

When having a cover designed, make sure you or the artist have rights to any photos used

Final Thoughts on Independent Publishing

Some authors love the challenge of creating beautiful books with POD. The myriad available options these days allow you more choices, and many of the platforms come with templates and possibly online options to build your book on their site. I personally love Atticus for formatting interiors. The software does most of the hard parts and lets you explore your creativity.

Although I usually dissuade people from using stock cover templates, you can use them for the base, but change the colors, pictures and whatever else you can to make it look unique. Or hire a cover designer to work with you for original cover art.

Rather than pay a company to do all the work for you, consider working with individuals who know the industry well to assist with all the parts. Many editors provide consulting to help walk you through the process, and with online tutorials, you may be able to complete the entire project.

Know your limitations, and get help where you need it. The best advice I received about publishing independently — have the book professionally edited and don't use a stock cover. You want your book to stand out from others, so the cover must be amazing. Learn all you can about creating the best ones if you plan on doing it yourself. If you need to hire professionals for the interior and cover, you can. Just make sure you choose wisely and that the one you hire has experience with POD.

PODs aren't self-publishing companies. They are platforms where you upload your book. Most require separate files for a print book, e-book, and covers for each. When I began the publishing journey years ago, only a few existed. I worked first with Lulu Press. They aren't my favorite, although Lulu remains a viable option. KDP (owned by Amazon) changed the landscape of POD. I still use them, but I also use IngramSpark and Draft2Digital (see websites below). These three sites offer print and e-books. If you want hardcover, Draft2Digital doesn't offer that yet. If you own the ISBN (which I recommend), you can upload files to multiple sites and even work on selling direct. You can also look at sites such as Bookvault, Bookbaby, Barnes & Noble, and others. Some of these sites offer help, but if it doesn't have a platform that allows you to upload yourself, you aren't on a POD site.

Jot down any questions you have about Independent Publishing.

Last Thoughts

Prepare to market like crazy so people know about your book – that's true regardless of the way you publish, no matter which path God takes you down on the way to seeing your book in print. Listen to His guidance as you make this important decision. And yes, you can start in one direction and change paths later if necessary.

You can do this. Stand firm and persevere to birth your book baby.

Do you feel more secure in knowing publishing options at this point? What would help you feel better informed?

_____

_____

_____

_____

_____

_____

_____

_____

What questions do you have unanswered after this lesson?

_____

_____

_____

_____

_____

_____

_____

_____

_____

_____

_____

_____

_____

_____

Lesson 8 Homework:

1. Look at several traditional publishing sites, find guidelines, and record any questions or insights you gain.
2. Search at least two of the POD sites and record questions and insights.
3. Create a list of possible publishing options for your book.

Bonus: Write a query letter and work on a proposal.

Suggested Resources:

(Note: these are a few websites to search for predators and other information related to publishing. Above all, seek direction and discernment from the Lord and ask questions of other writers.)

www.thechristianpen.com (Christan editors)

www.the-efa.org (Editorial Freelance Association)

www.facebook.com/prededitors/

www.writingcorner.com/preditors-and-editors/

www.sfwa.org/other-resources/for-authors/writer-beware/

www.stevelaube.com/who-owns-whom-in-publishing/

www.christianwritersmarketguide.com/

www.kdp.com

www.ingramspark.com

www.draft2digital.com

www.kindlepreneur.com/book-publishing/

www.writersdigest.com/getting-published/how-to-write-the-perfect-query-letter

Book Proposals That Sell by W Terry Whalin

www.blog.reedsy.com/guide/book-proposal/how-to-write-a-book-proposal/

The Sword and a Pen

12 Lessons for Christian Writers

"People can't read a book if they don't know it exists. All authors need to do marketing, regardless of how they published." ~Jo Linsdell

"The truth is, you could write a masterpiece, but if you're hiding it under a rock, no one will ever know." ~Bethany Atazadeh, *How Your Book Sells Itself*

Lesson 9—The Business Side of Writing

Focal verse for lesson 9: "Commit your works to the Lord and your plans will be established." (Proverbs 16:3 NAS95).

See also Matthew 25:14-30.

Lesson 9 Introduction

Some writers never truly learn the business side of writing. Few instructors talk about it. But when you publish a book, sell an article, story, devotional, or any other writing, you become a business owner by default. With that responsibility, writers must understand how publication affects them, and what parts of business they need to know.

Disclaimer: While I have an accounting background, I'm not an accountant, nor a tax specialist, nor an attorney. If you want or need more information, please consult with a professional in these fields.

What does the Bible say about business? I love Proverbs 16:3. When we commit our business to the Lord, He establishes us. In the same way we commit our writing to Him, we need to commit the business side of writing to Him.

The parable of the ten talents shows us God's view on business. He desires that we remain faithful with whatever He gives us. Use wisdom in business, but don't ignore something, expecting it to take care of itself.

Throughout the Bible, we find verses about honesty in business. The Lord demands that from us. Paul wrote to the Romans. "Pay to all what is owed to them; taxes to whom taxes are owed, revenue to whom revenue is owed, respect to whom respect is owed, honor to whom honor is owed." (Romans 13:7 ESV).

As entrepreneurs, we must follow this sound advice and the commandments throughout the Bible. But we also need to understand other aspects of writing and selling our writing if we want to succeed. While we may not expect to become millionaires from writing, remember this point. Those who show faithfulness with little receive more. As writers, we commit our work to the Lord, and He honors us with income. The way we handle it shows our love for Him.

We will touch briefly on a few things you need to consider as a published writer. Then we'll dig into marketing, because that seems to be the biggest void in the life of writers.

Business

1. Don't let the idea of becoming a business owner intimidate you. After all, we constantly hear to treat your writing as a job (AKA sit down and work on your manuscript every day). If we did this, we'd already have our first drafts.
2. Consider filing a dba.
    a. In Hood County, filing a business name costs around $20 and lasts for ten years when you can renew it if desired. It can be a person's name or get creative. You may want to check URLs (more later) for the name you choose. If you choose self-publishing this most likely becomes your publisher name.
    b. While not required for a writer, I highly suggest doing this.
3. Open a separate checking account. You will use this for income and expenses related to your writing business. To use a business name, you need the dba.
4. If you plan to sell books directly, apply for a Texas Resale Certificate. It costs nothing. You can wait until you're ready to sell in person, but it allows you to collect and pay state sales tax. Many writers never do this. They ignore state sales tax laws. If you don't sell much, it may never cause problems. But I always think about Paul's words, and I do it as the right thing to do.
5. Determine a way to track sales and expenses. Expenses may include the cost of books, Internet access, website costs, and a host of other things. Research what you should track. This will come into play when filing a tax return. You can legally and honestly offset income

from writing with these expenses. Obviously, if you make little money, this isn't a big issue.

6. Consider creating or having someone create a website for you. To start, you can go with something simple and build your own. That may be all you ever need. Pay for the URL so you have a unique place for fans to visit. While some businesses choose a FB page, keep in mind Facebook can cut you off. A website you purchase by the year, belongs to you.

7. Set up social media sites as desired. We'll touch on this in the marketing segment.

8. Learn about small business operations in Texas.

9. For self-publishers, strongly consider purchasing ISBNs through Bowker (www.bowker.com). Bowker is the official ISBN Agency for publishers (including self-publishers) physically located in the US and its territories. While you may see ads for purchasing from other companies, understand that the owner of the ISBN becomes the publisher of record.

    a. Having personalized ISBNs allows you to publish on multiple platforms and fully own your books in all formats you create.

    b. One ISBN costs $125. Ten costs $295. You can buy 100 for $575. And if you plan on becoming a super prolific writer, 1000 costs $1500. When you consider that one book in various formats (ebook, print paperback, hardcover, audiobook, large print, etc.), you could use four or five on one book.

10. Research copyright law (www.copyright.gov). Determine whether you want to register a copyright for your book. *Note: When you create any art, US copyright automatically covers your work, even if you don't register it.*

These ten bullet points may not include everything about the business setup of writing, but they capture much of the questions I had over the years. I learned by trial and wish someone told me more than the first few points.

What questions do you have about the general business side of writing?

_____
_____
_____
_____
_____
_____
_____
_____
_____
_____
_____
_____
_____
_____
_____
_____

Now that we have an idea about some of the tidbits of owning a business as a writer, let's dive into marketing. Because few writers enter the industry thinking like business owners, most don't approach marketing. We might throw a few things on FB, Instagram, LinkedIn, or other social sites, but as we talked about during our lesson on publishing, we need to market our books. How else will anyone know our masterpieces exist?

I can't begin to cover all the marketing strategies available. Honestly, if I had money, I'd say hire a PR firm or book marketing expert. But if you don't have a budget to do that, it helps to know something about this whole marketing thing. The resource list will have websites and possible book recommendations, but we'll try to cover a bit here.

Responsibility for Marketing

If you have a publicist or marketer, they'll handle most of your marketing needs. However, you still own a huge piece of telling people about your book. And most of us won't have experts working on our behalf, which is why we need to learn and do what we can. As our first responsibility of marketing, seek wisdom from Holy Spirit. Next, enlist our fans to help with this aspect of business.

Media Kit

What is a media kit? This "kit" includes everything someone needs to determine whether to interview us, invite us to speak, choose our book for a book club, to write an article, or any other publicity you want. In today's world, we can provide a folder with information about us and our book, or we can send an electronic file that contains everything we'd put in a three-prong folder with pockets. By using links, we can send prospective buyers to a book trailer or a PDF or ePub copy of our book. Once compiled, we can email kits to newspapers or other interested parties.

What does a media kit include? Visit "Media Kit Components," www.texasradicalwriters.com/wp-content/uploads/2023/11/Media-Kit-Components.docx.

If you have only one thing for your books, create a one-page that presents the description for your book, where to purchase it (preferably a single link), a short bio about yourself, and contact information. You can send this one-page document by email or snail mail, or post on social media. Get as creative as you want without distracting from the content.

The media kit allows an author to show creativity in many ways. Although it may sound a little intimidating, you can have fun putting it together and you might find a hidden talent along the way.

Email Lists

Keep your reader in mind. Ever have a conversation where the other person only talks about himself or herself? Do you want to have another conversation with him or her? Probably not. People want to gain something from relating to you.

When you send an email, make it about your reader. These are people who already said they want to connect. But what do they gain from you? Above all, protect your distribution list. You can do this best by having an email list through a third party, such as MailerLite, Mailchimp, Constant Contact, etc., which also includes the option to unsubscribe. Not that we want anyone to unsubscribe, but we must give them the opportunity to stop receiving emails from us for any reason.

If you have a website, you can link it to your mailing list, and when you post something, it goes out automatically by email. Or you can use that list for an email blast. Ideally, you provide content for your fans who sign up for your blog, newsletter, or both. Then you build a relationship with your followers, and of course, when releasing a new book, they become the first to hear about it. Ideally, they can't wait to purchase a copy and tell all their friends.

While we can also use social media for this same purpose, an email list belongs to you. If FB or X suspends your account, they can't touch those who signed up as contacts through your website or blog site.

In building the relationships, provide regular content for your readership. Include things they want to read about, not just all about you or your books. For example, I can provide a recipe the characters made in my novel. Or I can share secrets of pruning roses. I can reach out with seasonal greetings. By building relationships, I may also gain readers.

Social Media

Facebook, Instagram, X, Pinterest, LinkedIn, YouTube, TikTok, etc. So many to choose from. Years ago, writing gurus said set up all these accounts. We obediently did and then promptly ignored two-thirds of them. Social media can steal time from writing. Pinterest can suck you in, where you stay there for hours. Facebook can consume an entire day. Frankly, we don't have time for tons of social media — not if we keep writing books, articles, etc.

But these make great places to launch books, let people know about our newborn, and try to revitalize toddlers and even those school-aged books we birthed years ago. These days, the experts say choose one or two, maybe three of your favorite social media sites. Use them, but don't let the rest consume you. If you use only one, use it to the maximum potential.

On social media, as with email, build relationships between books. If all someone ever sees is a post begging them to buy your latest book, they are less likely to respond favorably. Give them content between books that let them know you and that seeks to know more about them.

Remember, it's not all about you.

Ads and Other Paid Marketing

You can purchase advertisements from Amazon, Facebook, and dozens of places. Newspapers and magazines might give you a brief press release spot, but they don't normally feature your book—unless they write an article or you pay for space. They love promoting your book with paid advertising. And you can choose that route if you want.

Free publicity is always best, but you can support local organizations by advertising your book on a program, t-shirt, etc. Keep in mind, you can spend little or a lot, depending on your marketing budget.

Many podcasts search for authors to interview, and they don't charge you to appear on their "show." Direct sales marketing happens at book fairs, author events, arts and craft fairs, and so many other places. Set up a book signing and create flyers from your one page. You may want these professionally printed.

See the resources below for sites you can research to learn more about marketing.

Book Launches

To launch or not to launch? Well, by default, when you release a book, you launch it. So that answers the question. But in all seriousness, how big of a launch should you do for a first book? For subsequent publications?

Because we celebrate every book we write, shouldn't we plan a launch party to some degree for every book we write? I suppose if you become a big-name author, you might forego a formal launch. Then again, we always need to let fans know we have a new title available.

Obviously, holding a launch party can help your book succeed. Since 2020, many authors lean toward online launch parties, and that can work if you have enough online followers. Some people love that type of book launch, while others love throwing a party.

Much depends on you as the author. The way you launch your book depends on your personality. What works best for one author may not work for others. Whatever you choose, plan well in advance if you want to have a successful book launch. An official launch marks the beginning of your marketing efforts, so don't miss this important step. See the resource list for a few articles on launching a book.

Brainstorm

As our last part of this subject, let's take a few minutes to brainstorm marketing ideas. Let's think creatively. Write down ways to market your book we have yet to discuss during this course.

_____
_____
_____
_____
_____
_____
_____
_____
_____
_____
_____
_____
_____
_____
_____
_____
_____
_____

Lesson 9 Homework:

1. Make a list of any business-related actions you feel led to pursue.
2. Write down marketing ideas you want to try for your book.
3. Brainstorm potential book launch ideas. Write down your favorites.

Suggested Resources:

www.texasradicalwriters.com/wp-content/uploads/2023/11/Media-Kit-Components.docx
www.authormedia.com
www.blog.reedsy.com/guide/blurb/
www.kindlepreneur.com/book-press-release/

www.ingramspark.com/blog/book-launch-checklist
www.blog.reedsy.com/book-launch/
www.writersdigest.com/publishing-insights/18-ideas-successful-book-launch

Beyond the Bookstore: How to Sell More Books Profitably to Non-Bookstore Markets by Brian Jud

If you conduct an online search for book marketing or book launches, you may find many more ideas. Tons of books and articles exist on this subject. Read but don't get so inundated you feel intimidated by it all. And remember, you can't market a book you have yet to write. Keep your focus where it belongs, but keep the business side of writing in mind, too.

The Sword and a Pen

12 Lessons for Christian Writers

"Publishing is a business. Writing may be art, but publishing, when all is said and done, comes down to dollars." ~Nicholas Sparks

Alleged impossibilities are opportunities for our capacities to be stretched. ~Chuck Swindoll

The will of God is never exactly what you expect it to be. It may seem to be much worse, but in the end it's going to be a lot better and a lot bigger. ~Elizabeth Elliot

Lesson 10—Beyond Publishing Books

Focal verse for lesson 10: "The hands of Zerubbabel have laid the foundation of this house; his hands shall also complete it. Then you will know that the LORD of hosts has sent me to you. For whoever has despised the day of small things shall rejoice, and shall see the plumb line in the hand of Zerubbabel. These seven are the eyes of the LORD, which range through the whole earth." (Zechariah 4:9-10 ESV).

Lesson 10 Introduction

When Jesus told the story of the talents (Matthew 25), Jesus said, "Well done, good and faithful servant. You have been faithful over a little. I will set you over much. Enter into the joy of your master. (Matthew 25:21 ESV). At times, we become entrenched in a massive, ultimate goal (AKA publishing a book). We forget about the small things—writing, editing, rewriting, proofing, etc. Each step of a book takes time.

Sometimes, while writing a book, you may become discouraged. While writers' block can haunt writers, we talked about the preparation and planning of books to help ease this phenomenon. Still, when working on an extensive project, you might want to write something that doesn't take days, weeks, months, even years. The long path to finishing a book well can get frustrating sometimes. And we talked about the resting period after finishing your first draft.

What do we do in those in-between times?

While many writers dream of a published book, we can pursue other types of writing. How can we extend our writing and use it to reach more people? What other publishing options exist for writers while working on a book or in place of a full-length project?

Some of the best writers don't start with books, and many never publish a book, yet influence more people than they ever imagined. If you have a book in mind, you can begin with smaller pieces of work or spend time simultaneously on them to break up the monotony or feel accomplished.

In addition, the world sees publishing as a business, and unfortunately, so do many traditional publishers — even in the Christian market. While we understand the business side of writing, that shouldn't be our main reason for writing. It differentiates Christian writers from the world.

Secular writers often pursue the writing of what sells best at the time. They "write to market." When God calls you to write and leads you in formulating an idea for a book, it may or may not fit the "market" when you start or finish the book. Ironically, Christians find that writing with the prompting of Holy Spirit may lead to a book like others which launch around the same time. As an editor, I see this many times. Multiple authors write about the same subject or something related within a time frame. I often read a manuscript that reminds me of a passage in another writer's manuscript or book. Amazing? Yes, but not really. God speaks and works constantly. How refreshing when we hear the same thing from Him and write books, articles, and more that complement each other.

Remember the why we discovered in lesson one? Take a minute to review why you write or want to write. In the space below, write your why again. Feel free to tweak it if necessary.

_____

_____

_____

_____

_____

_____

In remembering your why, can you meet that goal with something other than a book? Even while working on a book, we can prepare for the book's release with other avenues of writing besides preparing for marketing and all that other stuff. So, today, let's discuss what other writing we might consider. As always, these ideas may not cover everything out there, but it supplies starting points.

Articles (Paid and Free)

Writing articles provides a creative outlet for writers as well as publishing credits. Although you may spend time in the PITS (putting in time served) for articles when beginning, eventually you can make a fair amount of money from writing articles. Online e-zines, print magazines, etc. may or may not accept freelance submissions, so you may have to learn about query letters. Even if you use a market guide, be sure to check the publication's website for current guidelines and follow them exactly.

What do you write?

Experts say, "Write what you know."

When considering articles in magazines, target the magazines you read for a better chance of getting accepted. Learn interview skills and get a feel for what type of articles a publication uses. Learn the style of writing they like. While you don't want to lose your writer's voice, you want to adjust your style of writing to match articles they publish.

If you choose a secular publication, you can still weave in biblical truths. Writing for these publications gives Christians one of the best ways to reach non-believers, but it means learning to avoid terms you hear only in church. It may force you to perfect unique ways of phrasing these truths.

Devotionals

For Christian writers, taking time to write devotionals can prove rewarding, fun, and lucrative. Because most devotionals take little time to write, you can create several for submission. If accepted, the various companies pay $20 or more per piece. This also helps you learn the process of submitting your work for publication.

These devotionals might tie back to your book or not. They can be related to your life and the scriptures you read daily. Writing short daily devotionals not only provides publishing credits, but they also pay a little money, help establish your writing career, and normally require first rights. (See section below on rights.)

Also, consider writing daily devotionals as writing practice, self-discipline for writing, and a way to keep your focus on Jesus.

Copy Writing

Copy writing, sometimes referred to as copy editing, in the writing world means producing copy for websites, brochures, and other business materials. Often, this writing involves marketing skills to produce content that makes customers want to purchase products or hire a company for services.

Many writers enjoy this work, but others prefer not to pursue this type of writing. However, it can give a writer practice at back cover copy for books. Learn as many skills as possible before attempting this writing. Pay attention to what you see on websites, book descriptions, advertisements, etc.

While copy editing produces a fair amount of income, you may find it boring, and it seldom relates to your book content. Still, like any writing, copy writing hones writing skills. An excellent way to tighten writing, you generally need to produce information in as few words as possible.

Writers offer this service to people they know as a starting point. You build your business by word of mouth or by marketing your skills. Obviously, this grows as you improve and work with people. You may choose to work with Christians or non-Christians in pursuing this writing.

Blogs and Newsletters

If you write blogs, you are a published writer. Take advantage of blog posts. In today's world, they have less popularity than newsletters, but many people continue sending out weekly blog posts.

Like most other writing, the practice of writing blogs and newsletters helps improve skills and hones the discipline of regular writing. Blog posts or newsletters also help build email lists, which produce a way to market when you finish your book. By writing blogs or newsletters, you create relationships with your readers. When writing, always keep your reader in mind. The blog or newsletter is about them, not you. What can you provide the reader needs and wants?

This writing allows you to focus your reader more on the subject in your book. You can much more easily use this type of writing to relate more to what you plan to share in your book. Some people post blogs for months and then gather those posts to use as a book later.

When writing newsletters, the content varies depending on the writer and readership. Newsletters may contain a tidbit of knowledge about a subject, recipes, a verse, encouragement, inspiration, art, etc.

Often writers use blogs or newsletters to share a portion of their books, introduce a book cover, or seek feedback for a book or cover. The relationship building becomes the most important aspect of blogs and newsletters. Always leave the reader with an action, challenge or question, and hope for comments in return. You can post blogs to social media to draw people to your website, where they may enjoy more of your writing.

Short Stories and Anthologies

While writing a longer book, you may enjoy writing short stories or contributing to anthologies. *Chicken Soup for the Soul* books are one of the best-known anthologies, and many writers submit stories for various titles under the *Chicken Soup* umbrella.

Often writing groups or friends join efforts to produce an anthology. This practice requires at least one person who understands the publishing industry and can maneuver through the process. It also requires knowledge of interior and cover design or the willingness to pay for this service.

An individual who enjoys writing short stories may produce enough to create a short story collection. You can also find publications that accept freelance short stories, although you may need to query first. Again, visit the publication's website to determine current guidelines.

Other

Many authors collaborate with each other on book projects. The best advice I have for collaborative projects — create an agreement and have both parties sign it. No matter how well you know someone, an agreement puts in writing who will provide which part of a book. It also confirms the financial costs associated with the book. By putting these details in print, you avoid confusion and confirm expectations for all parties concerned.

Some writers spend time with ghostwriting. To best write for another person, you must spend an enormous amount of time with him or her. You must capture not only details of the story or book, but also the style of that person's voice. When you ghostwrite, the final manuscript sounds like the "author," not the ghostwriter.

As with collaboration projects, work under an agreement that specifies expectations and the fee charged for the completed manuscript, as well as any work promised following the completion of a manuscript. Many times, people hire a ghostwriter to complete their book, but they know nothing of the writing industry. They may expect the ghostwriter to complete a proposal and query or walk them through the self-publishing route. Be sure to understand what the client expects from you and who pays for any additional work or costs associated with completing the project.

As with most of our lessons, seek direction from Holy Spirit and follow the path He reveals to you. Trying to write in ways He never prepared for you to pursue may distract from writing what He desires most.

Although many writers seek writing-related projects for financial reasons, it takes self-discipline to continue with what God called you to write while working on other writing projects. Keep this in mind and determine a way to track everything. Make sure you have accountability partners for your primary projects.

Do any of these writing ideas appeal to you? If so, which ones and why?

_____

_____

_____

_____

_____

_____

_____

_____

_____

_____

Understanding Rights

When you submit content for publication, you sell or give away rights to use your writing. With a book, traditional publishers often require you to transfer your ownership of the copyright to them for a specified time (exclusive rights). When that time expires, or either side ends the contractual agreement, the rights revert to the author. With other types of publishing, make sure you understand who keeps the copyright. Obviously, when you publish your work independently, you retain all rights.

But what about other types of written content? You must understand this part of writing articles, etc. And all publications require or request various rights. You, as the author, determine which rights you offer. What are those rights?

All rights. When you give or sell all rights, that means you no longer own the copyright of the content. Copy writing normally falls under this type of rights. Publications such as *Guideposts* may request all rights. That means you cannot use the same content any other place. Be cautious when offering or agreeing to all rights. Unless the company pays well for your work, you may not want to agree. In addition, when you assign all rights, the new owner may resell your work without additional compensation. All rights may encompass electronic and other rights, too. Double-check a contract that seeks all rights.

The following paragraphs explain various rights you may give or sell to someone.

First rights or first serial rights. Agreeing to first rights allows a publication to use your content before anyone else publishes it. Only after they publish the content can you resell it elsewhere. Until they use what you wrote, you can't submit to someone else. If you produce content on a blog, you must share with a prospective publication you posted it on your blog. A magazine who requires first rights may not use content you previously published, even online. Many writers resell content to multiple magazines, reaping the rewards of writing once and selling many times. Not a bad idea if you need income from writing. Guidelines may also show the publication will not accept simultaneous submissions, so be sure you watch for this.

Onetime rights. When you sell onetime rights, you agree for a publication to use your content one time. This differs from first rights in that you don't have to wait for them to use your content before it appears elsewhere. Out of respect, make sure a publication that wants onetime rights knows if you submitted your work elsewhere. Not all publications accept this type of right — especially if they want to be the first to use the piece.

Reprint rights. After you sell work or publish it online, you can offer reprint rights. In this case, a secondary (or hundredth) publication can purchase and print your work, but you must share the original publication to honor your first rights agreement. Even if you simply blogged the content, you must say it first appeared on the name of your website or blog spot. Many publications don't want reprinted material, but some do. Be sure you check guidelines before submitting for reprint.

Exclusive rights. Book publishers frequently use this type of rights, but a magazine or other publication may request it, too. When agreeing to exclusive rights, be sure the offered contract details the specified amount of time they own exclusive rights. If not specified, address the period as an issue of a contract.

Electronic rights. When you sign over electronic rights, you allow a publication to use your content electronically. Audio or video rights may fall under "enhanced e-book rights," so make sure any agreement specifies the use of your copyright.

Subsidiary rights. This right allows the publisher to act on your behalf to license your work to others. With this agreement, make sure you understand compensation, otherwise you may give away the right and never receive additional income from your work while someone else does. Be cautious.

Worldwide rights. With worldwide rights, you give permission for the publication to translate and sell your work throughout the world. Many publishers may demand worldwide rights in addition to the other types. Again, make sure you understand the contract and compensation for this right.

Film rights. Obviously, if you give away film rights, you may end up making nothing from a blockbuster movie. Make sure you don't sign away film rights without specified compensation. [8]

Before signing a contract, even for a small article, story, poem, or any creative work, read carefully. If you don't understand the verbiage, seek feedback from an attorney — preferably one that deals with publications.

Lesson 10 Homework:
1. Choose a favorite magazine and search for writer guidelines. *(Hint: some magazines don't make it simple for writers, so you may have to tweak your search verbiage.)*
2. Practice a query letter for a magazine article.
Bonus: write and submit a devotional, query, article, or short story.

Suggested Resources:
www.christianwritersmarketguide.com ($9.99 annual online subscription or you can purchase a printed copy.)

www.pw.org/content/copyright#:~:text=first%20and%20second%20seria l%20rights%2C%20audio,versions%2C%20performance%20rights%2C%20 and%20merchandising%20rights.&text=first%20and%20second%20serial,r ights%2C%20and%20merchandising%20rights.&text=second%20serial%2 0rights%2C%20audio,versions%2C%20performance%20rights%2C%20and

www.writerswrite.com/journal/a-novice-writers-guide-to-rights-12977

www.writerbeware.blog/2023/04/14/rights-vs-copyright-untangling-the-confusion/

---

[8] (Poets&Writers 2023)

The Sword and a Pen

12 Lessons for Christian Writers

"Too often we underestimate the power of a touch, a smile, a kind word, a listening ear, an honest compliment, or the smallest act of caring, all of which have the potential to turn a life around." ~Leo Buscaglia

"No man can become rich without himself enriching others." ~Andrew Carnegie

"Alone, we can do so little; together, we can do so much." ~Helen Keller

Lesson 11—The Business Side of Writing

Focal verse for lesson 11: "As iron sharpens iron, so one man sharpens [and influences] another [through discussion]." Proverbs 27:17 AMP.

Lesson 11 Introduction

Don't you love this verse from Proverbs? During this course, you experienced the beauty of coming together as a group and learning the process of sharpening each other. At times, while learning a new skill, we may feel we receive all the sharpening and someone else provides the tool to sharpen us.

In all honesty, even those who teach often receive sharpening from their students. For teachers, the feedback can prove invaluable, and often the preparation for teaching a course pushes us to review and learn new concepts. Then those who learn also have insights we miss or forgot. Even questions help everyone in a group learn more. Never disregard your value as an important part of a small group. Whether you know everything, you certainly have experiences that help others.

I once heard a bestselling novelist state he didn't attend writing groups because he knew more than everyone there. With a master's degree in creative writing, he probably owned more knowledge than most of the people in the audience. His words prompted two thoughts in me. *1) If you have more knowledge, shouldn't you then be offering it to people in a group and help them grow? 2) Hmmm. Are you saying your life experiences exceed those of everyone in the group combined?*

Not daring to ask those questions out loud, I found his words arrogant and offensive. We all need community. Even the wise King Solomon recognized his need for friends to keep him sharp.

Interestingly, when I read this author's books, I came across a passage where he went into the description of a specific gun. He rambled for a full page or more, and I skipped most of it. It also made me realize how much I need fellow writers to hone my work. Had that author attended a writing group, someone might have had the guts to tell him to cut the description by 90%.

No matter how much knowledge or experience we gain during our writing journey, we need each other. Although writing requires time alone, we also need input to improve skills, check facts, watch for flubs, and to encourage us along the way. Plus, we need to give back and do the same for others.

In all areas of our lives, we often hear about networking. The influence of other Christians keeps us going when tempted to give up writing, and we need the accountability. The discussion of our work often makes it better than possible alone. With that in mind, let's talk about how we sharpen ourselves as writers.

Writing Groups

By attending regularly scheduled writing groups, you benefit in so many ways. First, knowing you'll meet with other writers often motivates you to continue working on your project. Accountability drives many authors to finish books, and these groups provide a means to achieve it. If you show up to a group with nothing, they may let you get away with it, but knowing they'll ask about your writing encourages your progress. That's one of the best benefits of meeting with other writers.

Second, you learn not only from the feedback on your manuscript but also as others read and receive feedback. Ideally, a group offers positive comments, highlighting what you did well and where you might improve.

Third, as you apply what you learn during a group session, you look at the entire work, not only the part you take to share. Because you continue writing, you also learn to hone skills during your rough draft and catch errors before finishing and going back to edit, which saves time long-term.

Fourth, writers understand other writers and the journey you travel. Friendships form among these groups, and you may find additional support from one or a few of the members who become some of the best friends. These people may become the ones who listen to future ideas for other books and offer insight. They also may be the friends who pray with you when writing gets tiresome and you want to quit. Treasure them.

How do you find a local group? Word of mouth, of course, works best, especially when you look for a like-minded group. Online searches or checking Facebook and other social media can help. Some local groups charge a minimum fee or meet for free. National or state organizations, such as the Texas Writers Guild, American Christian Fiction Writers, American Christian Writers, etc. normally have an annual fee, but they may offer more opportunities for learning and improving skills. While smaller, local groups offer a host of benefits, you may also want a connection to larger groups. You may join an online group as your primary group or a secondary one. You can belong to more than one group, but be cautious about spending more time meeting than writing.

As a leader of "encouragement and feedback" groups, I can attest to how much you learn from participating. You learn more when you lead groups, because what you don't know, you'll search to discover. As with anything, you get more by actively being part of the group and making it a priority.

In a group setting, remember, you don't have to make changes because someone in the group says so. Still, take the feedback and apply where needed. And don't feel intimidated because others in the group have more experience or more published work than you do. We all begin without publishing credits, although some may be farther down the road than you. Learn from them. And publication doesn't always mean that person knows everything. Listen to Holy Spirit as you receive feedback.

Most important, visit more than one group, if necessary, to find one where you fit. Not all writing groups fit every person, and you need one where the other members can give you the best feedback.

Conferences

Every writer should experience a conference—at least once. At conferences, you have multiple opportunities for learning. Some invite publishers and agents to attend, which can be a good way to land a traditional publishing deal if you want to try that route. Being among other writers can be exhilarating.

When looking for a conference (search online), consider the location, cost, what they offer, and what you can gain from attending. Many costs a considerable amount of money for the conference alone, and they don't include lodging. Major conference leaders negotiate special rates with nearby hotels, and some offer onsite lodging as a separate fee.

To lower costs for attending a conference, look for nearby ones so you can drive. One-day conferences may eliminate the need for staying in a hotel, and you can search for a B&B and share with other writers. Traveling and lodging together also help cover expenses, so consider that as an option.

As a Christian, understand that secular groups and conferences don't always share our values. With that in mind, look for the ones hosted by Christian entities. As with all things writing, seek Holy Spirit guidance to determine whether to attend a specific conference, not only for the content, but also as a good steward of the resources He provides.

If finances prevent you from attending, seek scholarships to conferences. Most offer them, and you may need to help in some area during part of the event. But it can be a way to attend.

Workshops and Seminars

Some groups offer a monthly workshop or special speaker. And with rising costs, organizations host special events as workshops or seminars instead of the more expensive conference method. As part of a group, you will hear of these events, but you can also watch online for events in your area. Social media may help find these, or you can search ticket-selling websites for them. Treat these as you would conferences, being selective in which you choose.

Workshops and seminars offer opportunities for learning, but typically on a limited basis. Some libraries host author events where you can attend for free and ask questions of various authors. As with conferences, these events can help you forge friendships with other writers. Search for local or nearby events to avoid the expenses of traveling. Look for groups, colleges, and libraries who host writing events. Low-cost workshops and seminars offer many benefits of a conference without the added expense of high-cost conference fees and travel.

Retreats

∞ **Corporate**

As conferences became more expensive, many groups opted for writing retreats. Since COVID-19, the popularity of writing retreats has grown, too. Often hosted by advanced writers or editors, this can be an acceptable option for writers.

Unfortunately, many of these retreats cost as much as a two- or three-day conference. In some cases, they become mini-conferences with little time for retreating. However, this can be a wonderful opportunity to get away and spend time with other writers, honing skills, and perhaps making time to work on your project.

For years, under Radical Writers (www.texasradicalwriters.com), I hosted biannual retreats. We continue to offer these in the spring and fall, but without all the instruction you find at other retreats. Instead, we choose a place near DFW where we go simply to write. If requested, we may have a session to improve skills in writing, marketing, or some technical aspect. Mostly, we retreat from the world to write — or relax and spend time in the Lord's presence.

∞ **Personal**

Although you can set aside a weekend or few days at home to focus on writing, life distracts us. Even those who live alone may find it difficult to ignore bulging trash, a sink full of dishes, or the need to do laundry or other tasks.

Seeking time away to write on a personal level may help with completing a project. Even though some live alone, they may need to spend a weekend away from home with nothing to do but write. Movies often place a writer in a cabin in the woods, which could be okay, but it doesn't have to be that venue. You might rather use time at the beach, a lakeside home, or simply in a hotel to get away from the mundane things of life and focus on a work in progress.

When retreating personally, try to avoid TVs and other distractions. Small towns work well for personal retreats, and often you can stay where nearby restaurants provide a meal and a break from writing. You may find a character for the current or another book in these places.

If you like city life, a hotel or B&B in a large city might work for you. Plan for extra days if you intend to see any tourist sights. You might also plan for an extra day or two when attending another event and turn that time into a mini-writing retreat.

A personal writing retreat can cause as little or as much as you want. Adventurous authors might pitch a tent in a state park and do some writing there. The beauty of a personal writing retreat allows a writer to choose where and when he or she wants to go. You also have only your schedule, not someone else's, and the budget you set. With a little planning and a lot of discipline, a personal writing retreat can result in fabulous progress on your work.

Accountability Partners

Finally, consider finding an accountability partner. This should be a writer who understands your style of writing and who will provide honest feedback. Most of the time, these partnerships go both ways. Be willing to share feedback as much as you receive and commit to the time you both select. The best partnerships consist of two writers who are on an equal level of writing or with one as the mentor and one as the mentee. While two novice writers might develop a wonderful friendship, they may not improve each other's skills. However, if this is your choice, it can work because you still hold each other accountable to complete what you promised.

To have a successful partnership for writing accountability, find a place where you can meet regularly and commit to the time you set. Share goals and progress, and if desired, you may critique each other's writing. Your times together work well for not only the accountability, but brainstorming future projects and simply encouraging each other.

Which of these networking opportunities most appeal to you?

_____

_____

_____

_____

_____

_____

_____

Which opportunities do you want to pursue over the next 6-12 months?

_____

_____

_____

_____

_____

As part of a writing group, what would you hope to gain?

_____

_____

_____

_____

_____

_____

_____

Lesson 11 Homework:

1. Select one or two of the opportunities you named in the above question. Search for local events to fit.
2. For fun, plan a personal retreat to get away and simply write. (Hint: in a busy season, your personal retreat might be a day at the library or in a local coffee shop.)
3. Consider ways to change your routine to accommodate your writing goals.

Suggested Resources:

www.angelo.edu/departments/english-modern-languages/writers_conference.php

www.acfw.com

www.blueridgeconference.com

www.thewritelife.com/attending-a-writers-conference-prepare/

www.writersdigest.com/publishing-insights/writing-group-best-practices-how-to-lead-a-successful-writers-group

The Sword and a Pen

12 Lessons for Christian Writers

"The Christian does not think God will love us because we are good, but that God will make us good because He loves us; just as the roof of a sunhouse does not attract the sun because it is bright, but becomes bright because the son shines on it." ~C.S. Lewis

"In almost everything that touches our everyday life on earth, God is pleased when we're pleased. He wills that we be as free as birds to soar and sing our maker's praise without anxiety." ~A. W. Tozer

"Do not strive in your own strength; cast yourself at the feet of the Lord Jesus, and wait upon Him in the sure confidence that He is with you, and works in you. Strive in prayer; let faith fill your heart-so will you be strong in the Lord, and in the power of His might." ~Andrew Murray

Lesson 12—Review

Focal verse for lesson 12: *"Don't be pulled in different directions or worried about a thing. Be saturated in prayer throughout each day, offering your faith-filled requests before God with overflowing gratitude. Tell him every detail of your life, then God's wonderful peace that transcends human understanding, will guard your heart and mind through Jesus Christ. Keep your thoughts continually fixed on all that is authentic and real, honorable and admirable, beautiful and respectful, pure and holy, merciful and kind. And fasten your thoughts on every glorious work of God, praising him always. Put into practice the example of all that you have heard from me or seen in my life, and the God of peace will be with you in all things."* Philippians 4:6-9 TPT.

Lesson 12 Introduction

Writing can produce stress in an author's life. How do we find time to finish writing projects, publish, and market them? We don't find time—we make it. Perhaps that increases the stress level though, because we live in a world with constantly full plates. But if God called us to write—whether it be one thing or a continued path for the remainder of our days—we'll find it challenging.

After all, we have an enemy who doesn't want us to walk in obedience to our calling. An enemy who doesn't want us to finish a book that might change a life or many lives. We face an enemy who wants anything but us walking in the fullness of all God planned when He created us. Sometimes, we need to acknowledge the truth—our battle isn't against flesh and blood, nor is it against busy days and nights filled with obligations and relaxation. And the best way to battle that enemy? Take everything to the Lord.

Regardless of the season, we find ourselves pulled in many directions. In spring, we long for time outside, maybe preparing a garden or simply breathing fresh air after months of confinement indoors. When summer arrives, we may consider vacations or we're so hot we can't think straight, and writing is the last thing we want to do. As autumn arrives, we again may venture outdoors, relishing the fresh breezes that cool rather than blow hot air in our faces. And toward the end of autumn, we move into the holiday season. As winter arrives, we might steal a moment because we're cooped up inside, hiding from the cold. But even then, we play catch up on the things we neglected all year, or we become entrenched in tax returns.

We can find excuses all year not to write. But we offer excuses—not valid reasons.

During the past 11 lessons, we spent time learning more about writing, improving skills, discovering the business side of writing and details about publishing and marketing. We now move into a season of applying all we learned, hoping to finish well. We need not fear moving forward. We can finish what we started because He who began a good work in us is faithful to complete it (Philippians 1:6).

As we continue in the writing process, remember this week's verse. If God called you to write something, He already knows your intimidation level. Admit it and don't neglect the thanksgiving part of the passage. Thank Him for all you now know, but didn't before. Thank Him for the desire to write and the strength and guidance He provides in this calling. Put into practice what you learned during this course, and depend on God to guide your writing.

He is faithful, and He never calls you to something without enabling you to do it. Take the smallest details to Him in prayer and see how He changes your writing life.

In this lesson, we'll review what you've learned. This is the time to ask questions and seek answers, plan to continue improving and writing. Find people to walk with you through this journey and believe God will bless the fruit of your hands and thoughts. Let Him work through you and may He continually bless you in ways beyond your wildest imagination.

What is the most important thing you learned during this course?

_____
_____
_____
_____
_____
_____
_____
_____
_____
_____
_____
_____

Review Questions and Discussion

Explore what you learned during this course. No right or wrong answers, record insights and questions arising from the content. Okay — maybe some of these questions have right answers, but focus more on exploring your mindset toward writing.

Answer questions with Holy Spirit by your side, seeking His will for your writing where applicable. Record any questions that arise during this review for further study or discussion with other writers. Use a notebook if you need more space.

As you work on this final lesson, feel free to go back and look through previous lessons for answers and your thoughts during those weeks. You've got this!

1. Reiterate why you write or want to write. Did your why change from lesson 1? If yes, explain how and why it changed.

_____

_____

_____

_____

_____

_____

_____

2. What do you see as next steps in writing?

_____

_____

_____

_____

_____

_____

_____

_____

3. How will you choose to let your writing reach hearts that need it most?

_____

_____

_____

_____

_____

_____

_____

_____

4. Define success in relation to your writing.

_____

_____

_____

_____

_____

_____

_____

_____

_____

5. Beside the W's of writing below, explain the importance of each one
   - What does the Bible say about writing?

   _____

   _____

   - Why do you write?

   _____

   _____

   - What do you write?

   _____

   _____

   - Who is your target audience?

   _____

   _____

   - When will you write?

   _____

   _____

   - Where will you write?

   _____

   _____

   - What place does Jesus take in your writing?

   _____

   _____

   _____

- Where do you start?

_____

_____

_____

6. What tool(s) did you choose for writing? Do you need additional training? If so, what do you need and how to you plan to learn more?

_____

_____

_____

_____

_____

_____

_____

_____

_____

_____

_____

7. Review Lesson Two and share your final concept summary in the space below.

_____

_____

_____

_____

_____

_____

_____

_____

_____

_____

_____

_____

8. What steps did you take to outline or plot your book? Did you complete at least one character sketch (fiction) or persona for your reader (non-fiction)? Do you need to take additional steps in preparation for writing?

_____

_____

_____

_____

_____

_____

_____

_____

_____

_____

_____

9. What research or other preparation do you need for writing?

_____

_____

_____

_____

_____

_____

_____

_____

_____

10. Do you need additional information to complete #8 or #9? If yes, what information do you need? How do you plan to learn more?

_____

_____

_____

_____

_____

_____

_____

11. What primary genre do you plan to write? (You can choose more than one.)

_____

_____

12. Part of POV (point of view) includes first, second, or third person. Draw a line between the type of person and example. Note: you may have more than one example for each type.

Butch glared at the intruder.

First Person

Give your best.

I ran to the door.

Second Person

You must read your Bible daily.

She skipped across the yard.

Third Person

We don't always understand complexities of writing.

Everyone answers the questions.

13. In third person or first person, you can also have *omniscient, distant,* or *deep* POV. Write the proper type beside each description below.

	All knowing, all seeing; typically feels like a narrator of the story who can see inside multiple characters, but not to any depth. Often promotes head-hopping, and can confuse readers at times.
	Seeing from one character's mind (often referred to as head), this type doesn't change perspective, but often feels more like telling a story instead of showing it.
	This type of POV stays in one character's mind and includes not only the action of a scene but the internal thoughts, emotions and perspective of that character.

14. Which POV do you think works best for your writing? (Hint: non-fiction may use second person, but you seldom see it in fiction. In non-fiction, if you include story, it should be first or second person although other parts of the book may be second person.)

_____

_____

_____

_____

_____

15. When writing fiction or creative non-fiction, how do you shift to a different character's POV?

_____

_____

_____

_____

_____

_____

16. "Without change you have no story. You only have a series of events." Ted Dekker. With this thought in mind, what is the overarching change in your story? (Hint: this generally involves your protagonist [main character], where he or she starts and what changes during the story.

_____

_____

_____

_____

_____

_____

_____

17. Briefly explain the difference between showing and telling a story.

_____

_____

_____
_____
_____
_____
_____
_____

18. In the below examples, place a T for telling or a S for showing in the blank before each sentence.

_____ It was a beautiful day.

_____ The wind raged against the house, boards creaking beneath the force.

_____ She responded in anger.

_____ Mickey walked across the plaza.

_____ Mickey sauntered through the plaza, smiling at the sky.

_____ Maddie was angry.

_____ She slammed the cabinet and whirled. A glint shooting from her eyes. "You'll pay for this."

19. What other questions do you have about the concept of show, don't tell?

_____
_____
_____
_____
_____
_____
_____
_____

20. Red flags of telling rather than showing include passive verbs, passages that sound flat, lack of emotion in a scene, etc. What other red flags can you name to help identify where you might be telling instead of showing?

_____
_____
_____
_____

_____

_____

_____

_____

21. The best dialogue sounds natural to the reader. The quickest way to kill natural dialogue comes from too many he said, she said tags. In the space below, write a short dialogue between two characters without adding dialogue tags.

_____

_____

_____

_____

_____

_____

_____

_____

_____

_____

22. When writing dialogue, going back-and-forth, don't forget to ground your characters so you don't end up with talking heads. In your dialogue from 21, what are some actions or observances you can add. For example: if the conversation happens in a coffee shop, what sounds might interrupt the dialogue?

_____

_____

_____

_____

_____

_____

_____

_____

_____

23. Match the types of edits with the definition by drawing a line between the two.

Copy Editing

Last step of editing before going to publications, looks for grammar, spelling, and typing errors. May included header and footer, chapter title style, etc.

Proofreading

Unique edit that falls between copyediting and developmental editing in intensity.

Content/Development/ Substantive

Broad and deep edit reviews all aspects of the manuscript. Less deep than content, development or line editing.

Line Edits

Encompasses overall improvement.

24. Which edits do you think you'll need when finished with your manuscript?

_____

_____

_____

25. Name the six common errors you can correct before sending to an editor for a professional edit.

26. Of the six items listed above, where do you need the most help with understanding, identifying, or correcting when self-editing?

_____

_____

_____

_____

_____

_____

_____

27. What is the first thing you should do after completing your manuscript?

_____

_____

28. Using the list on the left, place each in the proper order for what to do after you finish writing. Some steps may repeat or switch order.

Celebrate	
Rewrite and correct from edits	
Choose publishing option	
Self-editing	
Proofread and publish book	
Marinate	
Assemble Beta Readers & Launch Team	
Professional editing	
Celebrate and market that baby	
Create a marketing plan	

29. What are the three primary types of publishing available today?

_____

_____

_____

_____

_____

30. Name some pros and cons for each type of publishing.

_____

_____

_____

_____

_____

_____

_____

31. What is the most important thing to remember when researching publishers?

_____

_____

_____

_____

_____

_____

32. Which option appeals to you most at this point in your journey or which direction do you sense Holy Spirit leading? Why?

_____

_____

_____

_____

_____

_____

_____

33. As an author or published writer, your work automatically becomes a business. Does this thought intimidate you? Why or why not?

_____

_____

_____

_____

_____

34. What steps do you need to take in preparation for a writing business?

_____

_____

_____

_____

_____

_____

_____

_____

35. Who owns the responsibility for marketing a book, writing, or anything related?

_____

_____

_____

_____

36. In the section below, circle all items that may be part of a media kit.

Press release	Headshot	Author Bio
Printed copy of your book	Book trailer	Bookmarks
Book bio	Photo of author's kids	Testimonials

Another author's book	Target audience	Book excerpts
Cool hat	Comparable titles	Other books in series
Photo of author's cat	Interview questions	Story ideas for reporters
Downloadable author & book photos	Author information for contact	Scheduled dates for author appearances
Non-downloadable stuff	Author's best friend pic	Bribery payment

37. In addition to writing books, authors may choose to pursue other publishing opportunities. Many authors begin with other types of writing, and it may or may not earn money, but it produces publishing credits, which can prove invaluable when trying to build credibility. Consider the list below and indicate which you might pursue.

	Articles		Devotionals		Copy Writing
	Blogs		Newsletters		Short Stories
	Anthologies		Other (specify):		

38.

True   False   When you create any artistic work (writing or otherwise) the piece is automatically copyrighted even if you don't register it.

39. Match the copyright definitions with types.

Note: Understanding rights protects a writer from financial and emotional risks. Before signing a contract, make sure all rights requested include compensation clauses. If needed, seek a publication attorney's advice.

First rights/first serial rights	All-inclusive, everything to do with the work.
Onetime rights	After initial publication, someone else may print the content again, noting where first published.
Reprint rights	The right to act on your behalf and license your work to another entity.
Exclusive rights	The right to produce your work as a film.
Electronic rights	Use of content before anyone else publishes, this right allows the author to resell to other publications only after the original printing.
Subsidiary rights	Allows a publication to use the content only once. Doesn't require waiting for publication.
Worldwide rights	For a specified time, the holder of this right is the only one who can print your material.
Film rights	The right for publisher of your content to translate into various languages.
All rights	The right to use your content in a digital format.

40. Iron sharpens iron. Which is the easiest, least expensive way to sharpen writing skills?

_____

_____

_____

_____

41. When looking at potential writing conferences, what four things should you consider?

_____

_____

_____

_____

_____

_____

42. What type of workshops or seminars would most interest you as a writer?

_____

_____

_____

_____

_____

_____

43. If you attended a personal or corporate writing retreat, what would you want to accomplish during that time?

_____

_____

_____

_____

_____

_____

44. On a writing retreat, which would you prefer? (Circle as many as you want.)

    a. Nothing but writing.
    b. Only teaching with little or no time for writing.
    c. One or two hours of teaching with most of the time spent writing.
    d. Fun activities that have nothing to do with writing.
    e. Lots of rest and relaxation.
    f. Some rest but also time set aside for writing.
    g. Other (specify):

_____

_____

_____

45. Name at least one person you would consider approaching as a writing accountability partner. This may be a reader or prayer partner and not necessarily a writer. However, a writer can hold you accountable and help improve skills or allow for brainstorming a work in progress.

_____

_____

_____

As we wrap up this review of *The Sword and a Pen*, do you feel confident in continuing this journey of writing?

Consider all you've learned. Don't let it intimidate you. We covered much ground during our weeks together. Use this book as a resource and return to it often. As your skills improve, you will need it less, although we always need reminders to write well.

While you don't have to obtain all the recommended resources, make a list of ones you most want to own. Add them to wish lists for birthdays, Christmas, and other special holidays, adding them over time. These become valuable tools of your trade.

Most importantly, seek Holy Spirit in all you write, knowing what God called you to write, He will enable you to finish. Find a verse that reminds you of that call, or ask Him to reveal one to you. Write it down and keep it where you can see it during those times when you want to quit. Because those times will arise, but that's when your writing buddies prop you up and encourage you to keep writing.

Finally, commit to let Him who began this good work in you complete it. Whether you write one thing or follow this journey of writing for the remainder of life, know He who gifted you to write and gave you the desire empowers you to give it the best you can. Be faithful to use that gift as He directs you.

Now, pick up your SWORD and let it guide you in God's way to use your pen.

References

Cameron, Julia. 1992, 2002. *The Artist's Way.* New York: Penguin Putnam, Inc.

Chesson, Dave. 2023. "Writing Point of View: 1st, 2nd, 3rd & 4th POV (with Examples)." *Kindlepreneur.* July 17. Accessed September 22, 2023. https://kindlepreneur.com/point-of-view/.

Jenkins, Jerry B. 2017. "A Writer's Guide to Point of View." *Jerry Jenkins.* November 14. Accessed September 22, 2023. https://jerryjenkins.com/point-of-view/.

Littauer, Florence. 1989. *Silver Boxes: The Gift of Encouragement.* Nashville, TN: Thomas Nelson.

Littauer, Marita. 2023. "Wired That Way: The Personalities." *The Personalities.* July 27. https://thepersonalities.com/category/the-personalities.

Mathis, David. 2017. "God Made You a Writer: An Invitation to Every Christian." *Desiring God.* August 17. Accessed August 19, 2023. https://www.desiringgod.org/articles/god-made-you-a-writer.

Poets&Writers. 2023. "Copyright Information for Writers." *Poets&Writers.* Accessed November 19, 2023. https://www.pw.org/content/copyright#:~:text=first%20and%20second%20serial%20rights%2C%20audio,versions%2C%20performance%20rights%2C%20and%20merchandising%20rights.&text=first%20and%20second%20serial,rights%2C%20and%20merchandising%20rights.&text=second%2.

Reedsyblog. 2020. "The Ultimate List of Book Genres: 35 Popular Genres, Explained." *ReedsyBlog.* December 29. Accessed September 6, 2023. https://blog.reedsy.com/book-genres/.

Lisa Bell

About the Author

Published author of fiction and non-fiction books, Lisa Bell worked as a community editor for NOW Magazines, LLC from October 2015 until January 2023, credited with hundreds of articles. She enjoys encouraging writers, helping improve skills, and offering expertise for independent publishing with technical skills for editing, interior design, and custom covers.

A leader of two writing groups (see www.texasradicalwriters.com) plus a small group for writers at The Heights Church, Granbury, Lisa speaks or teaches whenever the opportunity arises. She holds a BS in Business Management from the University of Phoenix, is a CLASS alumnus, and a panelist for The Writers View (www.thewritersview.groups.io). Single mother and grandmother, she lives southwest of Fort Worth, TX where she volunteers in her community and strives to always learn new things. www.bylisabell.com.

www.ingramcontent.com/pod-product-compliance
Lightning Source LLC
Chambersburg PA
CBHW041141120626
46547CB00020B/3070